# FINISH LINE

## Writing

### for the Common Core State Standards

Continental

# Acknowledgments

**Illustrations:** Page 149: Laurie Conley

**Photographs:** Page 7: NASA; Page 17: Tony Weller; Page 21: www.istockphoto.com/Eric Bechtold; Page 25: www.shutterstock.com, Darren Hubley; Page 31: www.shutterstock.com, Galina Barskaya; Page 40: www.istockphoto.com/Maica; Page 46: Image used under Creative Commons from HenryK Kotowski; Page 76: Image used under Creative Commons from David Shankbone; Page 85: www.shutterstock.com, Mandy Godbehear; Page 114: ©Royalty-Free/Corbis; Page 134: www.photos.com; Page 143: ©Royalty-Free/Corbis; Page 179: Adam Crowley; Page 181: www.shutterstock.com, Ronald Caswell

ISBN 978-0-8454-6768-8

# Table of Contents

# Welcome to Finish Line Writing for the Common Core State Standards

This book will give you practice in the skills necessary to be an effective writer. It will also help you prepare for writing tests that assess your skills and knowledge.

The material in this book is aligned to the Common Core State Standards for English Language Arts and Literacy in History, Social Studies, Science, and Technical Subjects. The Common Core State Standards (CCSS) build on the education standards developed by the states. The CCSS "specify what literacy skills and understandings are required for college and career readiness in multiple disciplines." This book will help you practice the writing skills necessary to be a literate person in the 21st century.

In the lessons of this book, you will review the writing process and then apply those skills in different types of writing. You will also read informational and literary selections and then answer multiple choice, short-response, and extended-response questions related to them and to the application of writing skills. The lessons are in three parts:

- The first part introduces the writing skill you are going to study and explains what it is and how you use it.

- The second part is called Guided Practice. You will get more than practice here; you will get help. You will read a nonfiction passage and answer questions about it. After each question, you will find an explanation of the correct answer or a sample answer. So you will answer questions and find out right away if you were correct. You will also learn why one answer is correct and others are not.

- The third part is Test Yourself. Here you will read a question and then write an answer on your own.

After you have finished all of the lessons and units, you will take a Practice Test at the end of the book.

Now you are ready to begin using this book. Good luck!

# Elements of Writing

Do you think of yourself as a writer? You are! And you probably know a lot about writing. You know it takes creative thinking and good organization. You also know that not all writing is the same. When you take a writing test, for example, your time is limited. When you write a research paper, you have several weeks to work on your writing. This unit is about the steps in the writing process. It is also about the elements that make up good writing.

- **In Lesson 1,** you'll review the five steps of the writing process: prewriting, drafting, revising, editing, and publishing. You can use this process in all the writing you do.

- **In Lesson 2,** you will focus on what makes a strong paragraph. The paragraph is the main building block of any writing you do.

- **Lesson 3** is about the main idea and supporting details in a text. This lesson will help you identify the main idea and learn how to support it or explain it with details in your writing.

- **Lesson 4** focuses on how to structure your writing using cause and effect. This type of organizational structure is best used for connected events. It helps the reader understand what happened and why it happened.

- **In Lesson 5,** you'll learn about another organizational structure. This lesson focuses on comparing and contrasting two things to show how they are alike and how they are different.

# The Writing Process

**W.5.4–6**

Writing is a process—something you do in steps. Most writers follow five steps:

**Prewriting → Drafting → Revising → Editing → Publishing**

An easy way to remember the writing process is to think of what you do in each step. In the prewriting step, you **plan** what you will write. The drafting step is when you actually **write.** After that, you go back for the **revising** step. Once you are satisfied with the draft, the next step is **editing** what you have written. Finally, you **publish** your writing.

## Step 1: Prewriting

In this prewriting step, you plan what you will write. To start, you need to think about the following:

**Read**
Note
Organize

- Why you are writing (your purpose)
- What you will write about (your subject)
- What you will say (the content)
- How you will say it (your voice)
- Who will read it (your audience)

Sometimes, however, you are writing for a test. Then some of these things are already decided for you. For example, read this question from a test.

> <u>Robots</u> like C-3PO and R2-D2 in the *Star Wars* movies are very different from the robots that exist in real life today. Write an article for your <u>school newspaper</u> that <u>compares and contrasts</u> the robots of science fiction movies with real robots.
> In your article, be sure to include:
> - how science fiction robots and real robots are similar
> - how they are different

This question tells you the purpose (to compare and contrast), the subject (robots), and the audience (the students in your school). The rest is up to you. You need to work out the content—what information you will present and how you will organize that information. Many writers begin by underlining the important words as above and jotting down notes.

Read
**Note**
Organize

Sometimes it helps to use a graphic organizer when you are planning your writing. For this assignment, you might use a comparison and contrast chart like this one.

## Robots

### What's Different?

**Movies**

- They look and act more like humans than machines.
- They are programmed to do things like translate languages and deliver secret plans.
- They can be loyal friends.
- C-3PO has "creativity circuits," which allow him to tell stories.

**Real Life**

- They look more like machines than humans.
- They do work that is boring or dangerous.
- They don't really have feelings or emotions.
- They have artificial intelligence, so they can do things like move around objects and pick things up.

### What's the Same?

They are mechanical devices.

They are designed to do work that is usually done by humans.

They replace humans in certain kinds of jobs.

For different types of writing, other graphic organizers like these may be helpful.

- **Cluster map or web**—This organizer can help you get your ideas on paper for many kinds of writing.
- **Venn diagram**—A Venn diagram can help you organize your ideas when you want to compare and contrast two things.
- **Sequence chart**—A sequence chart is best when you are writing a narrative. It helps you map out events in the order they happen.

# Guided Practice

> Your school has activity clubs as part of its afterschool program. Your principal is asking for ideas of activity clubs that it could add to the program. School rules state that any such activity must be educational. Write a proposal describing one activity that you would like to have as part of the program. Explain what the activity is. Provide enough details to show why it would be educational.
>
> In your composition, be sure to:
> - explain your activity
> - explain why it would be educational

Who is the audience?

**A** students

**B** principal

**C** club leader

**D** afterschool program coordinator

The audience is not the students, club leader, or afterschool program coordinator. Choices A, C, and D are incorrect. The correct answer is choice B. The audience is the principal who will decide what activity clubs should be added to the afterschool program.

What is the purpose of the writing assignment?

_____

_____

Think about what you want to accomplish with your letter. Here is a sample answer:

The purpose of the writing assignment is to propose educational activities to add to afterschool programs.

**UNIT 1** ▨▨▨▨▨▨▨▨▨▨▨▨▨▨▨▨▨▨▨▨▨▨▨▨▨▨▨▨
Elements of Writing

What type of graphic organizer could you use to organize your writing?

A   web

B   Venn diagram

C   cause and effect chart

D   sequence chart

 A Venn diagram is used to compare and contrast two things. A cause and effect chart shows relationships. A sequence chart shows the order of events. Choices B, C, and D are incorrect. These are not the best choice to plan a persuasive argument. Choice A is the correct answer.

## Step 2: Drafting

After you have planned what you will write, it's time to put your ideas into sentences and paragraphs. This step is **drafting.** Don't worry about spelling and grammar at this point. You can change things later. The important thing now is to write down your ideas.

There are two ways to draft what you want to write. One is to brainstorm or free write. This is when you just start writing, letting your ideas move forward. This works well for some writing tasks. You can write as you think about what you want to say. However, you will probably need to spend a lot of time revising what you have written.

The other way is to work from the prewriting plan you made. This is much easier because you have organized most of your ideas about what you want to write. Make sure you have a clear main idea and that you support it with details. Each paragraph should have its own main idea. Use transitions and a strong conclusion. Here is a draft that could be written based on the comparison and contrast chart on page 7.

Robots in movies look and act more like humans then machines. Real robots look more like machines then humans. R2-D2 and c-3PO, the robots in the Star Wars movies, have lots of human characteristics. They feel loyal, and form friendships. They do things like translate langauges and deliver secret plans. R2-D2 can only beep and whistle. C-3PO even has creativity circuits that enable him to make up stories.

The real robots we have today are more like smart machines. They have artificial intelligence and can do jobs in factories. They do dangerous work like handling toxic materials and defusing bombs. You can buy a robot vacuum cleaner. It's a flat oval machine that moves over the floor. It senses where dirt is and goes there to suck it up. When its done, it goes back to it's base.

The robots in sci-fi movies and real robots have some things in common They do work that is normally done by humans and can replace humans in certain kinds of jobs.

## Step 3: Revising

Once you have finished your draft, the next step is **revising.** In this step, you read what you have written and make changes to improve your work. You make sure that what you have written is clear to your readers.

When you revise, you might need to change the content of your work, or you might want to rework its structure. Asking yourself these questions can help you decide what changes you should make to improve what you have written.

### Content
- Does my writing have a main idea?
- Have I included enough supporting details?
- Is there any place where I should add an important detail or example?
- Have I included details that are not important and should come out?
- Does my writing have an introduction and conclusion?

### Structure
- Is my writing organized in a way that fits the topic?
- Are my relationships between my ideas clear?
- Do I need to add words, phrases, or sentences to make them clearer?
- Do my sentences clearly express the point I want to make?
- Are my sentences well written?

# Guided Practice

The robots we see in movies often make us think that robots are science fiction and there are no robots in real life. That is not true. There are robots today, but they are not exactly like the robots we see in movies.

Robots in movies look and act more like humans then machines. ~~Real robots look more like machines then humans.~~ R2-D2 and c-3PO, the robots in the <u>Star Wars</u> movies, have lots of human characteristics. They ~~feel~~ are loyal, and they form friendships. They do things like translate langauges and deliver secret plans. ~~R2-D2 can only beep and whistle.~~ C-3PO even has creativity circuits that enable him to make up stories.

Real robots look more like machines than humans. ~~The real robots we have today are more like smart machines.~~ They have artificial intelligence and they can do jobs in factories. They robots do dangerous work like handling toxic materials and defusing bombs. There are also robots that do household chores. You can buy a robot vacuum cleaner. It's a flat oval machine that moves over the floor. It senses where dirt is and goes there to suck it up. When its done, it goes back to it's base.

The robots in ~~sci-fi~~ science fiction movies and real robots have some things in common They do work that is normally done by humans and they can replace humans in certain kinds of jobs.

Why did the writer add the first paragraph?

Think about what the reader needs to know when reading a text. What information did the new paragraph give the reader? Here is a sample answer:

The draft needed an introduction.

Why was a sentence moved from paragraph 2 to paragraph 3?

Think about the structure of the text. Consider what the reader needs to know first, second, and last. Each paragraph has a main idea that needs to be made clear to the reader. Here is a sample answer:

The sentence is in the wrong place. It is the topic sentence for paragraph 3. It talks about robots as machines, not ones in movies.

Why was a sentence taken out of paragraph 2?

Each paragraph has a main idea. The rest of the sentences in the paragraph support that main idea. Some sentences provide important details and information that support the main idea. Some sentences provide details that are unnecessary or unrelated to the main idea. Here is a sample answer:

This sentence is not an important detail.

## Peer Review

Sometimes for class writing assignments the teacher might have students work in pairs to edit each other's papers according to a rubric. Then the students can review the comments and revise their work accordingly. This is known as **peer editing** or **peer review.**

When writing for a test or a classroom assignment, you may receive a rubric that lists what is expected for a range of scores. Sometimes one

**UNIT 1** ░░░░░░░░░░░░░░░░░░░░░░░░░░░░░░░░░░░░░░
Elements of Writing

rubric is used for the whole writing task. Other times two rubrics are used. A score is given for topic development, ideas, organization, and use of language. Another score is given for the use of standard English—how well you observe the conventions of sentence structure, grammar, and capitalization. Rubrics for writing may differ but they should look something like the one below.

## SAMPLE RUBRIC

**Score 3**

- The writing answers all parts of the question.
- There are at least two clear comparisons and two clear contrasts.
- Transitional words and phrases connect the ideas.
- Each paragraph has a topic sentence that clearly states the subject.
- Supporting details are organized in a logical order.
- The writing is easy to read and stays on the subject.
- There are almost no mistakes in grammar, capitalization, punctuation, and spelling.

**Score 2**

- The writing answers almost all parts of the question.
- There are two generally clear comparisons and two contrasts.
- Transitional words and phrases connect most ideas.
- A topic sentence stating the subject is missing or unclear.
- Some supporting details are missing or are not in a logical order.
- The writing is fairly easy to read and mostly stays on the subject.
- There are some mistakes in grammar, capitalization, punctuation, and spelling.

**Score 1**

- The writing answers only part of the question.
- There are fewer than two comparisons or two contrasts.
- Very few transitional words and phrases are used to connect ideas.
- More than one topic sentence is missing or unclear.
- Many supporting details are missing and are not in a logical order.
- The writing is not easy to read or is off the subject in many places.
- There are several mistakes in grammar, capitalization, punctuation, and spelling.

# Step 4: Editing

When you have revised your work and are happy with it, the next thing you do is **edit** your work. This means that you reread what you have written and check that everything is right. You look for mistakes in grammar and usage. You also look for mistakes in spelling, capitalization, and punctuation. You edit to make sure that

- subjects and verbs agree
- pronoun forms are right
- punctuation marks are used correctly
- all words are spelled correctly
- names are capitalized
- titles are underlined or in quotes

To edit your revision, you first go over it sentence by sentence, and mark the places that need correcting. This is called **proofreading.** When you proofread, you use some of these marks to show your changes.

| Proofreading Symbols | |
|---|---|
| ∧ Add letters or words. | List ideas ^about^ your topic. |
| ⊙ Add a period. | That is not true ⊙ |
| ≡ Capitalize a letter. | R2-D2 and c̲-3PO are loyal. |
| ⊂ Close up space. | They form friend⌒ships. |
| ⋏ Add a comma. | There are robots today‸but they are different. |
| / Make a capital letter lowercase. | The R̸obots today are different. |
| ¶ Begin a new paragraph. | ¶ Real robots look like machines. |
| ⨍ Delete letters or words. | Real robots look like re⨍al machines. |
| ∿ Switch the position of letters or words. | The robots are today like machines. |

# Guided Practice

**Practice using proofreading marks with this paragraph.**

Real robots usual look more machines, than humans.  they have artificial intelligence can do jobs in Factories  They do dangerous work handling like toxic materials and defusing bombs.

Did you find all the errors? Here are the corrections:
Sentence 1: Delete the word *usual*. Add the word *like* after the word *more*.
Sentence 2: Capitalize the word *they*. Insert the word *and* after the word *intelligence*. Lowercase the word *Factories*.
Sentence 3: Transpose the words *like* and *handling*.

Read the draft below with its proofreading corrections. Circle the corrections in the draft below.

The robots we see in movies often make us think that robots are science fiction and that there are no robots in real life. That is not true. There are robots today, but they are not exactly like the robots we see in movies.

Robots in movies look and act more like humans ~~then~~ ^than^ machines. ~~Real robots look more like machines then humans.~~ R2-D2 and c-3PO, the robots in the Star Wars movies, have lots of human characteristics. They ~~feel~~ ^are^ loyal, and ^they^ form friendships. They do things like translate ~~langauges~~ ^languages^ and deliver secret plans. ~~R2-D2 can only beep and whistle.~~ C-3PO even has creativity circuits that enable him to make up stories.

Real robots look more like machines than humans.
~~The real robots we have today are more like smart machines.~~
They have artificial intelligence ^and^ can do jobs in factories. They ^robots^ do dangerous work like handling toxic materials and defusing bombs.

*There are also robots that do household chores.*
You can buy a robot vacuum cleaner. It's a flat oval machine that
moves over the floor. It senses where dirt is and goes there to suck
it up. When ~~its~~ *it's* done, it goes back to ~~it's~~ *its* base.
*science fiction*
The robots in ~~sci-fi~~ movies and real robots have some things in
common. They do work that is normally done by humans and *they* can
replace humans in certain kinds of jobs.

 Were you able to find all eight corrections? Some are misspellings and others are missing punctuation. Here are the corrections:

Paragraph 2
　Change the word *then* to *than*
　Capitalize the letter *c* in *c-3PO*
　Change the word *langauges* to *languages*
Paragraph 3
　Insert a comma after *artificial intelligence*
　Change the possessive *its* to the contraction *it's* in <u>when its done</u>
　Change the contraction *it's* to the possessive *its* in <u>back to its base</u>
Paragraph 4
　Insert a period after the word *common*
　Insert a comma after the words *done by humans*

## Step 5: Publishing

　Once you are satisfied that you have corrected any errors or problems with your work, you are ready to publish it. Publishing means to make your work public and share it with others. This is the final form that your readers will see. Publishing can take many forms. You can share your work with friends or family. Or, you can post it on a bulletin board or include it in a class booklet. Another way to publish your work is to post it on the Internet in a blog or on a website. You can publish your work in a slideshow. Publishing can also mean just turning your work into your teacher or writing it on a test.

# Test Yourself

> Which is a better way to watch a movie, at home or at the theater? Write an essay that compares and contrasts the two ways to watch a movie.
>
> When writing your essay, be sure to do the following:
> - follow all the steps of the writing process
> - tell how the two ways are alike
> - tell how the two ways are different

1 To understand what the question is asking, look for key words and underline them. Write the key words below.

_____

_____

Read
**Note**
Organize

2 What type of graphic organizer would you use to organize your ideas?

A web

B timeline

C Venn diagram

D cause and effect chart

Read
Note
**Organize**

**3** Now that you have thought about the topic and have organized your
ideas, write a draft of your essay. Your draft should explain how the
two ways to watch a movie are alike and how they are different.

_____

_____

_____

_____

_____

_____

_____

_____

_____

_____

_____

_____

_____

_____

_____

_____

_____

_____

_____

_____

_____

_____

_____

**4** When you have written your draft, reread it carefully. Then revise the content and structure if they need to be changed. Finally, edit your revision for spelling, punctuation, capitalization, and grammar. Use the rubric on page 13 to review your writing.

_____

_____

_____

_____

_____

_____

_____

_____

_____

_____

_____

_____

_____

_____

_____

_____

_____

_____

_____

_____

_____

_____

_____

**5** Then write your final answer on the lines below. Show your essay to your teacher. Or, exchange papers with another student. Review each other's writing, and give it a score based on the rubric. Discuss ways you can each improve your writing.

_____

_____

_____

_____

_____

_____

_____

_____

_____

_____

_____

_____

_____

_____

_____

_____

_____

_____

_____

_____

_____

_____

_____

**UNIT 1** ❊❊❊❊❊❊❊❊❊❊❊❊❊❊❊❊❊❊❊❊❊❊❊❊❊❊❊❊❊❊❊❊❊❊❊❊❊❊❊❊
Elements of Writing

# Writing a Paragraph

### W.5.4–6

The paragraph is the basic building block of everything that you write. Most of the things that you read or write are made up of several paragraphs. Each paragraph focuses on one topic or main idea. The sentence that explains the main idea of the paragraph is the **topic sentence.** This is often the first sentence in a paragraph. However, it does not have to be the first sentence. The other sentences in the paragraph support the topic sentence. They do this by providing more information or details about the main idea. The last sentence ends the paragraph by making a **conclusion.**

## Guided Practice

**Read the paragraphs. Then answer the questions.**

Some people wonder why there are still trains in this age of aviation. Trains are an important part of the transportation network across America and around the world. They move both people and things from place to place. Often, trains carry freight to major trade centers. The freight cars are then moved to trucks that take them to specific destinations. People can also make both short and longer journeys by train. Train travel is slower, of course, than flying, but there are other benefits. Trains are often more comfortable, and train travel is less expensive. Trains are going to be with us for a long time.

What is the topic sentence in the paragraph?

_____

_____

_____

 First, determine what the paragraph is about. The topic of the paragraph is trains. The topic sentence tells you the main idea of the paragraph. In this paragraph, you are going to read about why trains are still important. Here is a sample answer:

> The topic sentence is the second sentence. "Trains are an important part of the transportation network across America and around the world."

Have you ever played video games? _____ _____.They can be played on a game system connected to the television, or they can be played on a computer. Video games have been shown to help students learn strategy and think logically. Professions from medicine to the military use video games to train people. Video games help them learn techniques they have to use in real life.

What is the topic of the paragraph?

A computers

B medicine

C learning

D video games

 The paragraph is about video games. It discusses how they can be played on computers. The paragraph explains that they are used to train people in medical and military fields, and they can help people learn. Choices A, B, and C are incorrect. The correct answer is choice D.

Write a topic sentence for the paragraph.

 Your answers will vary. However, the topic sentence should note that video games are used by many different people. Here is a sample answer:

*Video games are popular with people of all ages.*

## Organizing the Paragraph

A good paragraph makes sense. Every sentence should be about the topic. The sentences should be in some logical order. Here is a flow chart that shows how the paragraph about trains on page 21 is organized by details.

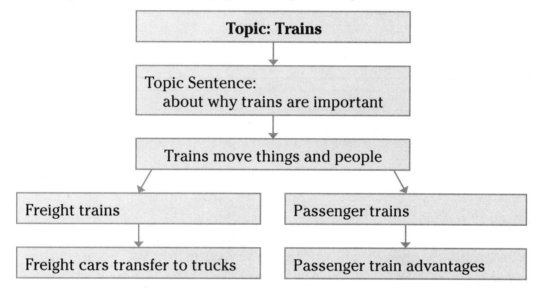

The paragraph is about trains. The topic sentence explains why trains are important. The paragraph then discusses the two types of trains: freight trains that move goods and passenger trains that transport people. Then the paragraph gives details about these two types of trains. The paragraph then ends with a closing sentence about trains.

If you are writing just one paragraph, you should end with a closing sentence or conclusion. The closing sentence ends a paragraph and makes a **conclusion** about the topic. "Trains are going to be with us for a long time" is the closing sentence in the paragraph about trains.

# Guided Practice

Older streetcars and trolleys ran right down the middle of the street.

Light rail transit systems are today's version of the streetcar.

Light rail systems in cities usually run on the side of the road.

There are light rail systems in cities, between towns, and from cities to suburbs.

Like streetcars, light rails run on electricity, and they do not pollute the air.

_____

_____

_____

_____

_____

_____

First, decide which sentence is the topic sentence. Next, number the sentences in order. Then use this order to write the sentences in the form of a paragraph. Finally, write a concluding sentence. You should develop your paragraph according to the way you ordered your sentences. Here is a sample answer:

> Light rail transit systems are today's version of the streetcar. Like streetcars, light rail systems run on electricity, and they do not pollute the air. Older streetcars and trolleys ran right down the middle of the street. Light rail systems in cities usually run on the side of the road. There are light rail systems in cities, between towns, and from cities to suburbs. The modern light rail system is a clean and efficient form of mass transit.

There is more than one way to organize a paragraph. The order you choose depends on the type of writing you are doing. Here are some other ways to organize information in a paragraph.

When you write a paragraph, you often want to explain something. You can do this in two ways. You can follow your main idea with **details** that support it, as the paragraph about trains on page 21 does. Or, you can organize your paragraph so that **examples** support the main idea. This is what the paragraph on streetcars does.

When you write a story or personal narrative, you should use **time order** or **sequence.** In a story or narrative, you need to tell the events in the order that they happened. Transition words and phrases help you put events in time order. These include words like *first, then, after, later,* and *finally.*

Sometimes you must write an answer to a question on a test. These questions may be called **brief or short responses.** Your answer should be a paragraph. Test-taking time is limited, but you can follow these steps to write your answer.

1. Underline the key words to be sure you understand the question.
2. Think about what you want to say.
3. Decide which organizational plan you will use.
4. Write your topic sentence first, and then finish your paragraph.
5. Check your answer. You can still make changes.

## Guided Practice

**Read this passage about computers. Then answer the questions.**

### Computers Are Everywhere

The age of technology has reached into the everyday lives of American families. Over 85% of families with children now have computers. Computers are used for everything from playing games to shopping to paying bills. Many children do their homework on computers, and they surf the Internet for fun as well as for information for schoolwork.

People who do not have a computer at home still use them in many places. Most schools have

computers available for their students to use. Many local libraries have computers for their customers to use as well as for information about the books on the shelves.

Many jobs require people to use computers. Of course, offices use computers. Salespeople and deliverers use computers to keep track of their work. If you decide to apply for a job at the supermarket, you may use a computer to fill out your application. And, if you get the job, you will use a computer when you work. Learning to use a computer is a basic skill for everyone these days.

> Do you use a computer for schoolwork, for playing games, or for communicating with friends? Write a paragraph about an experience you have had using a computer.

_____

_____

_____

_____

_____

Here is how one student, Kayla, wrote her answer to the test question. First, she underlined important parts of the question and made some notes. She knew she would need to write a narrative, or a story, about her own experience with computers. She decided to use time order to organize events in her story.

**Read**
**Note**
Organize

To plan her writing, Kayla wrote down the events that she wanted to tell. Then she arranged them in the order in which they occurred.

 Here is what she wrote:

1. Ava emailed me last Saturday

2. She wanted to play a computer game

3. I learned how to play the week before

4. We began to play

5. She taught me tricks

**Read**
**Note**
**Organize**

6. I improved and beat her

7. I stopped playing to have dinner

8. After dinner I called her to thank her

9. We decided to play the next day

Once she completed her plan, Kayla used the events she listed to write her short response in the form of a paragraph.

 **Kayla's paragraph follows her sequence of events. Here is what she wrote:**

Last Saturday afternoon my cousin Ava, who lives in Utah, emailed me. She wanted to play a computer game with me. She had been practicing the game for three months. I had just learned to play the week before. We both logged on and began to play. While we were playing, she showed me a lot of new tricks. By the end of the afternoon, I had improved so much that I actually beat Ava in one game. My mom finally made us stop playing so I could have dinner. After dinner I called Ava to thank her for helping me improve. We made plans to play again the next day.

What words did Kayla use to show time order?

_____

_____

_____

 **Think about the sequence of events. What words are clues to when events happened? Here is a sample answer:**

Kayla used these words: Last Saturday afternoon, for three months, week before, while, By the end of the afternoon, finally, After dinner, the next day.

What is Kayla's topic sentence?

_____

_____

 The topic sentence tells the reader what the paragraph is about. Here is a sample answer:

Kayla's topic sentence is "She wanted me to play a computer game with her."

What is Kayla's concluding sentence?

_____

_____

 A single paragraph often ends with a conclusion. The conclusion sums up the paragraph. Here is a sample answer:

Kayla's concluding sentence is "We made plans to play again the next day."

# Test Yourself

1  Which is *most likely* the topic sentence of a paragraph about kites?

   A   The tail of a kite can be short or long.

   B   A kite can be made from a kit or from materials around the house.

   C   Flying kites is a very popular hobby among children as well as adults.

   D   Some kites are shaped like diamonds, while some have triangular shapes.

2  Which is *not* a supporting sentence in a paragraph about football?

   A   The football field is divided into ten-yard segments.

   B   Football is one of the most popular sports in the United States.

   C   To score in football, you need to reach the end zone with the ball.

   D   The Super Bowl is football's final championship game in the United States.

3  Which is *most likely* the topic sentence of a paragraph about sleep?

   A   Sleep is a critical part of staying healthy.

   B   Children need the most sleep to help their bodies grow.

   C   People sleep in 90-minute cycles that repeat many times each night.

   D   When you sleep, your brain and body recharge so you have energy the next day.

4  Identify the *most likely* topic sentence of a paragraph about vegetables.

   A   Vegetables are usually low in calories.

   B   Vegetables are usually full of essential vitamins.

   C   A serving of vegetables is usually a half cup, raw or cooked.

   D   Nutrition studies recommend three to five servings of vegetables daily.

**5** Read the question. Then write your response.

> The passage on page 26 ends with the conclusion that "Learning to use a computer is a basic skill for everyone these days."
>
> Explain what the writer means by this statement. Be sure to include a topic sentence that states your main idea. Support your topic sentence with your own examples or by using details or information from the passage.

_____

_____

_____

_____

_____

_____

_____

_____

_____

_____

_____

_____

_____

_____

_____

_____

_____

_____

_____

_____

_____

**UNIT 1**
Elements of Writing

# Main Idea and Details

W.5.2, 4–6, 8, 9

The **main idea** is what a text is about. The main idea can usually be expressed in one sentence. Details support or explain the main idea. When you write a paragraph, the main idea of the paragraph is called the **topic sentence.** The other sentences in the paragraph support the main idea.

## Guided Practice

**Read the passage. Then answer the questions.**

### The Story of Arbor Day

In 1854, J. Sterling Morton and his wife settled in the Nebraska Territory. Not long after moving into their new home, they noticed that something was missing. There were no trees. The Nebraska landscape was mostly treeless plains. The Mortons knew that trees would prevent soil erosion and provide shade. They soon planted trees around their own property. Morton began to write newspaper articles to encourage other people to plant trees, too.

When Morton became secretary of the Nebraska Territory, he decided to do something about the lack of trees. He proposed a tree-planting holiday, and he called it Arbor Day. On the first Arbor Day in Nebraska over one million trees were planted. In 1885, Nebraska made Arbor Day a legal holiday and set the date for April 22, Morton's birthday. Other states soon followed with their own Arbor Days. Before long, the tradition of planting trees on Arbor Day had taken hold across the country.

Today most states observe Arbor Day on the last Friday in April, which is also national Arbor Day. Some states have Arbor Day at a different time when the weather is better for planting trees. No matter what day it is celebrated, tree planting on Arbor Day has become a beloved tradition. It is celebrated in many countries around the world.

A grove of shade trees near your neighborhood is going to be made into a park with benches and picnic tables. It will be named Morton Park after J. Sterling Morton. Write an article for your neighborhood newsletter explaining who J. Sterling Morton was and why the name is appropriate for the park. In your article be sure to include:

- a main idea about why the name is appropriate
- facts and details from the article that support the main idea

## Step 1: Prewriting

Here's how one student, Azizah, used facts and information from the passage to write an answer to the question. Azizah knew it was important to read the question more than once. She underlined the important words and made some notes.

**Read**
**Note**
**Organize**

What important words do you think Azizah underlined? Explain why you think she underlined these words?

_____

_____

_____

_____

_____

Before you begin to write, you need to understand the purpose, the audience, the content, and the length. Here is a sample answer:

Azizah underlined <u>article</u> because this is what she is asked to write. She underlined <u>newsletter</u> because this tells her where the text will appear. It helps her understand how to structure her text. She underlined <u>main idea</u> and <u>facts and details</u> because these are important elements that she must include in her text.

Azizah also made some notes to help her with her writing. Here are her notes:

> topic—J. Sterling Morton
> audience—neighbors
> Morton started Arbor Day
> A million trees were planted the first time
> Other states started Arbor Day
> It's a national day now
> It's even in other countries
> People plant trees every year

She noted *what* the topic is and *who* her audience is. She also wrote down the main idea of the article and facts and details.

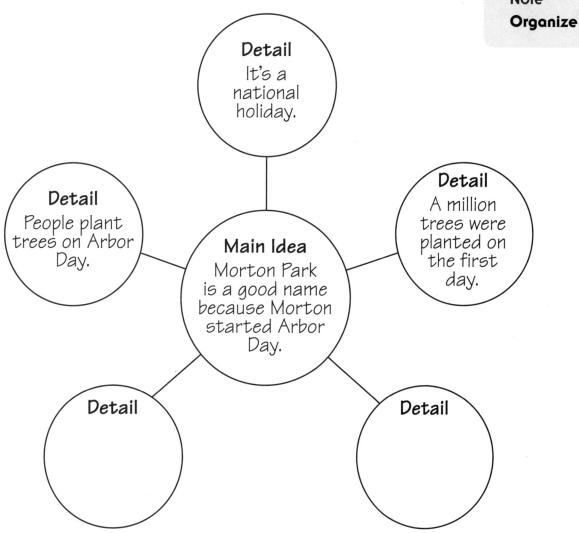

What two details that support the main idea would you add to the graphic organizer?

 The details should relate to Morton and why he planted trees on the plains. Here is a sample answer:

Morton and his wife loved trees. Morton knew that trees provide shade.

Azizah's next step was to write her draft.

## Step 2: Drafting

**Read the draft. Then answer the questions.**

Morton Park is the perfect name for our new neighborhood park. It's the one with the lovely grove of shade trees. The name "Morton" means J Sterling Morton. This is the person who started Arbor day, which is a special holiday for planting trees.

Morton started Arbor Day because his wife and he loved trees. When he moved to Nebraska, they found there were no trees where they lived. There was just a plain He knew that trees were needed because they provided shade. They liked seeing the flowering trees, too. When he became Secretary of the Nebraska Territory he had Day declared a holiday. He hoped that some would plant trees on that day. On that first Arbor Day in 1872, over a million trees were planted. Arbor Day is still celebrated today. Arbor Day is now a national holiday. People from all over the world also celebrate this day. And plant trees. We should name our park after Sterling J.

**UNIT 1** ✖✖✖✖✖✖✖✖✖✖✖✖✖✖✖✖✖✖✖✖✖✖✖✖✖✖✖✖✖✖✖✖✖✖✖✖✖
Elements of Writing

Morton because of his love of trees. It is a good way to honor J.

Sterling Morton, and we should name our park after him. Thanks to

him, the world today has more trees.

What is Azizah's topic sentence?

_____

_____

 **The topic sentence gives the main idea of a paragraph. Here is a sample answer:**

"Morton Park is the perfect name for our new neighborhood park."
This is the topic sentence.

What is the most important detail that Azizah has included?

_____

_____

_____

 **You must be able to distinguish between important and unimportant details when writing. This helps you know how to structure your paragraph and support your main idea. Here is a sample answer:**

"The name 'Morton' means J Sterling Morton. This is the person
who started Arbor day, which is a special holiday for planting trees."
This detail explains and supports why Morton Park is a good name
for the new park.

The next step is for Azizah to revise what she has written.

# Step 3: Revising

Morton Park is the perfect name for our new neighborhood park.
~~It's the one~~ with the lovely grove of shade trees. The name "Morton"
<u>honors</u>
~~means~~ J Sterling Morton. <sup>He</sup> ~~This~~ is the person who started Arbor day,
which is a special holiday for planting trees.

Morton started Arbor Day because his wife and he loved trees.
<sup>they</sup>
When ~~he~~ moved to Nebraska, they found there were no trees where
they lived. There was just a plain He knew that trees were needed
because they provided shade. ~~They liked seeing the flowering trees~~
~~too.~~ When he became Secretary of the Nebraska Territory he had
<sup>people</sup>
Day declared a holiday. He hoped that ~~some~~ would plant trees on
that day. On that first Arbor Day in 1872, over a million trees were
planted. Arbor Day is still celebrated today. <sup>and</sup> ~~Arbor Day~~ is now a
national holiday. People from all over the world also celebrate this
<sup>by planting</sup>
day. ~~And plant~~ trees. We should name our park after
Sterling J. Morton because of his love of trees. ~~It is a good way to~~
~~honor J. Sterling Morton, and we should name our park after him.~~
Thanks to him, the world today has more trees.

Why did Azizah cross out two sentences?

_____

_____

_____

_____

✓ Sometimes we revise for content. Here is a sample answer:

In paragraph 2, Azizah crossed out a sentence that was not an important detail.

In paragraph 3, she crossed out a sentence that was similar to the one before it.

Which sentences did she combine?

_____

_____

✓ Revising also includes rewriting to improve what you have written. Here is a sample answer:

Azizah combined the first two sentences in paragraph 1 and the first and second sentences in the last paragraph.

# Peer Review

Once you are satisfied with your draft, have a peer edit your work. Exchange papers with another student. Review each other's writing, and give it a score based on the rubric. Discuss ways you can each improve your writing.

## RUBRIC for Main Idea and Details

**Score 3**
- The writing answers all parts of the question.
- Each paragraph has a topic sentence that clearly states the main idea.
- The writing includes important details that clearly support the main idea.
- The writing is easy to read and stays on the subject.
- Words are used correctly and well.
- There are almost no mistakes in grammar, capitalization, punctuation, and spelling.

**Score 2**
- The writing answers almost all parts of the question.
- A topic sentence stating the main idea is missing or unclear.
- The writing includes some details that support the main idea.
- The writing is fairly easy to read and mostly stays on the subject.
- Some words are misused.
- There are some mistakes in grammar, capitalization, punctuation, and spelling.

**Score 1**
- The writing answers only part of the question.
- More than one topic sentence is missing or unclear.
- Many details are missing or they do not support the main idea.
- The writing is not easy to read or is off the subject in many places.
- Many words are overused or misused.
- There are several mistakes in grammar, capitalization, punctuation, and spelling.

The last step is for Azizah to edit what she has written.

# Step 4: Editing

Edit Azizah's draft on page 36 for five more mistakes. Write your corrections below.

_____

_____

_____

_____

✓ Did you find all the mistakes? Here is a sample answer:

In paragraph 1, there should be a period after the initial J and the word *day* should be capitalized.

Paragraph 2 should be indented. A period should be added after the word *plain*. The word *Arbor* should be added before the word *Day*.

# Step 5: Publishing

The final step is for Azizah to publish her paper. She can do this by using a computer to create her final paper and email it to her teacher. Or, she can handwrite her paper and turn it into her teacher.

# Test Yourself

## Directions for Planting a Tree

Are you planning to plant a tree this Arbor Day? Before you begin, you will want to learn the basics of tree planting. With planning and care, the tree you plant will survive and grow, giving you pleasure for years to come.

Before you begin, find out if this is the right time of year to plant a tree. Climate plays a big role in deciding when to plant. Newly planted trees do best with moderate temperatures and rainfall. Trees need time to develop roots and get used to the temperature before the heat of summer or the cold of winter begins. That's why spring and fall are usually the best time to plant a tree. In the southern United States, the warm winter means you can plant a tree any time of the year.

1.  Choose a tree that is right for your climate. Don't try to force a warm weather tree to grow in cold northern areas. Check with your local tree nursery for suggestions.

2.  After you have chosen your tree, you're ready to dig the hole. It should not be too deep or too narrow. The roots of the tree need room to spread out, and they need to be close enough to the surface to get oxygen. As a rule of thumb, never plant a tree deeper than the soil in which it was originally grown. The hole should be about three times the width of the tree's root structure.

3.  If your tree has a root ball wrapped in burlap, lift the tree by the root ball, never by the trunk. Remove the burlap and all string and twine from the root ball.

4.  Loosen the root structure with your hands. That will allow the roots to expand. Lower the tree into the hole.

5.  Mix fertilizer with good soil, following the directions on the container. Fill the hole, but do not compress the soil. If you do, water will not get to the roots.

6.  When the tree is planted, fertilize the soil around the planting hole to promote growth.

7.  Water the base of the tree well.

**UNIT 1** ▓▓▓▓▓▓▓▓▓▓▓▓▓▓▓▓▓▓▓▓▓▓▓▓▓▓▓▓▓▓▓▓▓▓
Elements of Writing

You have decided to give a tree to your friend in Georgia whose birthday is on Arbor Day. Write a note to your friend with suggestions for planting the tree. In your note, be sure to include:

- a main idea
- important details and information for planting a tree

**Read**

Note

Organize

**1** What kind of writing are you being asked to do?

_____

_____

_____

_____

_____

_____

**2** What will the structure of your writing look like when you are done?

_____

_____

_____

_____

_____

_____

**3** Who is your audience?

_____

_____

_____

_____

_____

_____

**4** Read the question again to see where to start your planning process. To give your friend clear instructions, you need to understand the main idea of the direction and important details.

Read
Note
**Organize**

The question tells you to provide steps for planting a tree. This means you need to identify the key idea in each step to write clear directions for your friend. Use the graphic organizer below to plan your writing.

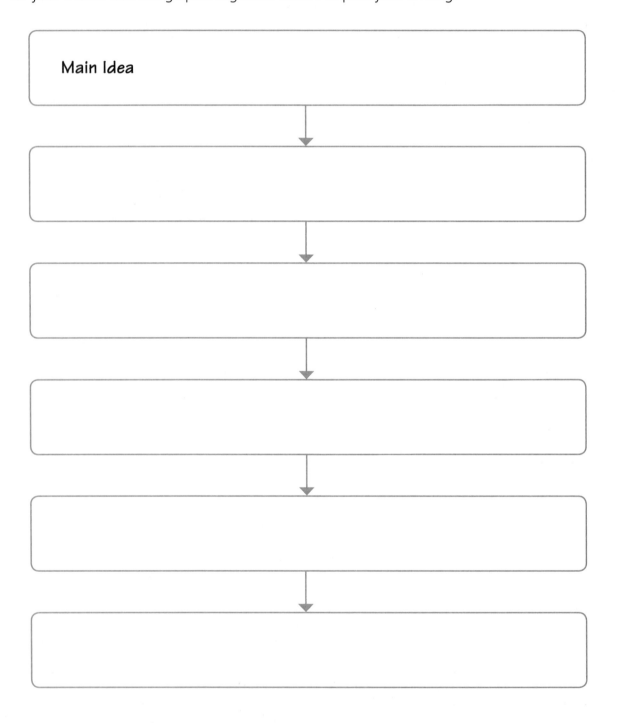

Main Idea

**5** Now it is time to write your draft. Before you write your draft, review your graphic organizer. Think about what your topic sentence should be. Are all your ideas in the correct order? Do you need to add details to make the process clearer? Remember to clearly state the main idea and use supporting details to let the reader know why you have included the information in each step.

_____

_____

_____

_____

_____

_____

_____

_____

_____

_____

_____

_____

_____

_____

_____

_____

_____

_____

_____

_____

_____

**6** Once you have finished your draft, go back over it. Make your revisions on this page. Then proofread your draft. Use the rubric on page 38 to review your own writing.

_____

_____

_____

_____

_____

_____

_____

_____

_____

_____

_____

_____

_____

_____

_____

_____

_____

_____

_____

_____

**7** When you are satisfied with your writing, you are ready to publish your work. Write your final copy on the lines below. Then show the paper to your teacher.

_____

_____

_____

_____

_____

_____

_____

_____

_____

_____

_____

_____

_____

_____

_____

_____

_____

_____

_____

_____

_____

_____

_____

# Cause and Effect

W.5.2, 4–6, 8, 9

When you read, you probably see connections between ideas and events. These connections explain why things happen. Your reading makes more sense when you understand these *why* connections. Look for clue words that signal **causes** *(because, since, due to)* and **effects** *(then, so, as a result)*.

## Guided Practice

**Read the passage. Then answer the question.**

### Student Uses Class Learning to Save Others

Teachers say that what you learn in class connects to real-life events. However, not every student understands the connection. English schoolgirl Tilly Smith understands the connection. She helped save more than one hundred people because she paid attention in class.

A tsunami struck the coastal areas of the Indian Ocean on December 26, 2004. Tsunamis are giant sea waves. Tilly was on vacation with her parents and younger sisters in Phuket, Thailand, when the tsunami hit. With its beautiful beaches and friendly people, Thailand is a popular winter vacation spot for tourists from Europe.

On the morning of the tsunami, Tilly and her family were sitting on Maikhao Beach. They watched as the tide rushed out, sucking water out to sea and away from the shore. Tilly noticed how bubbly and strange the water looked. This odd activity rang a bell. Just two weeks before,  her geography teacher, Mr. Kearney, had explained how an earthquake under the ocean can cause a giant sea wave, or tsunami. She also learned how the sea looks and acts before a giant wave hits shore. The class even saw a video of one.

**UNIT 1**
Elements of Writing

In a flash, Tilly realized that a tsunami, the subject that Mr. Kearney had been teaching was about to happen—right here and right now. No one else on the beach seemed to realize what was happening. She screamed at her mother to tell her what she knew and that they had to get off the beach. The Smiths yelled at the other tourists to run, and everyone raced up to higher ground and their hotel. All of the people on Maikhao Beach escaped the giant waves. They were incredibly lucky.

The people from Maikhao Beach have Tilly to thank for their lives. And who does Tilly thank? Mr. Kearney, her teacher.

> Write an essay telling why Tilly Smith was able to help people during the tsunami. Explain what experiences caused Tilly to recognize danger.
> In your explanation, be sure to include:
> - your main idea
> - two or more causes and their effect
> - transition words such as *because, since, so, as a result*

## Step 1: Prewriting

**Read**
**Note**
Organize

Here is how a student, Matt, used the information from the article to write the answer to a test question.

The first thing he did was to read the question carefully. Then he made a few notes to help him remember the key points of the question.

> what I will write about: how a girl saved people's lives
> how I will organize: cause and effect
> I must include: two or more causes and the effect
> my main idea
> transition words

The next step after reading the question is recognizing cause and effect relationships. For the question about Tilly Smith, Matt needs to find out how two or more events caused one effect.

After Matt identified the causes and effect, he decided to use a graphic organizer to make sure that the causes occur before the effect and that the effect follows in logical order. Matt made the chart below.

| CAUSE |
| --- |
| Tilly learned about tsunamis in geography class and even saw a video. |

| CAUSE |
| --- |
| Tilly saw the tide and the water that looked like the video. |

| EFFECT |
| --- |
| Tilly realized that a tsunami was coming and saved the people on Maikhao Beach. |

Matt looked over his graphic organizer. He decided to begin his answer by stating the effect first. Matt then listed his ideas and some details in the order he would write them.

Use the passage and graphic organizer to complete Matt's list.

1. Tilly saved people on Maikhao Beach from the tsunami. [effect]

2. Tilly saw the tide rush out and noticed that the water looked bubbly and strange. [cause]

3. _____

   _____

4. _____

   _____

5. All the people ran from Maikhao Beach and were saved from the tsunami. [effect]

 Matt noted after each sentence whether it was an effect or a cause. What other causes can you add to the list? Here is a sample answer:

Tilly told her mother what she knew. [cause]
Tilly and her mother warned the other tourists on
Maikhao Beach. [cause]

The next step is to use your graphic organizer or paragraph plan to write your draft. Begin your paragraph with a main idea sentence. It should state the cause or effect of your topic.

**UNIT 1** ▨▨▨▨▨▨▨▨▨▨▨▨▨▨▨▨▨▨▨▨▨▨▨▨▨▨▨▨▨▨▨▨
Elements of Writing

# Step 2: Drafting

Tilly Smith is an English girl who saved the lives of hundreds of people in Thailand because of what she learned in school. A tsunami is a gigantic sea wave. She was sitting on Maikhao Beach when she noticed something unusual. The tide rushed out from the shore and the water looked funny and strange

Tilly is just 10 years old, but she was the only one on the beach who understood what that meant. She realized what the sea was doing was a sign a tsunami was coming. Her teacher in England had just taught the students about tsunamis. What a story she would have to tell geography class!

She knew that a tsunami was very dangerous, so she told her mother what was happening and that they had to run from the beach. Then they quickly warned the other tourists on Maikhao Beach, and they all ran to safety. So, as a result of Tilly's quick thinking, hundreds of people escaped the tsunami.

Tell how this draft is organized by identifying the following:

Topic Sentence:

_____

_____

Cause 1:

_____

_____

Cause 2:

_____

_____

Effect:

_____

_____

✓ **The effect is what happens and the cause is why it happens. Here is a sample answer:**

Topic Sentence:
Tilly Smith is an English girl who saved the lives of more than one hundred people in Thailand because of what she learned in school.

Cause 1:
Tilly saw the tide rush out from shore and that the water looked strange.

Cause 2:
Tilly realized that a tsunami was coming.

Effect:
Tilly and her mother warned the other tourists about the tsunami, saving many lives.

Once Matt finished his draft, his next steps were to revise and edit the draft. A peer review can also be helpful once the draft has been revised. When the revised draft is completed, then it is time to edit the piece.

# Step 3: Revising and Step 4: Editing

Read the revised draft and answer the questions.

Tilly Smith is an English girl who saved ~~the lives of~~ hundreds of

people in Thailand ^from a tsunami because of what she learned in school. A tsunami

is a gigantic sea wave. She was sitting on Maikhao Beach when she

noticed something unusual. The tide rushed out from the shore and

the water looked ^bubbly ~~funny~~ and strange⊙

Tilly is just 10 years old, but she was the only one on the beach who

understood what that meant. She realized what the sea was doing

was a sign a tsunami was coming ^because Her teacher in England had just

taught her class about tsunamis. ~~What a story she would have to~~

~~tell geography class!~~

She knew that a tsunami was very dangerous, so she told her

mother what was happening and that they had to run from the

beach. Then they quickly warned the other tourists on Maikhao

Beach, and they ran all to safety. ~~So,~~ as a result of Tilly's quick

thinking, hundreds of people escaped the ^deadly tsunami.

UNIT 1
Elements of Writing
51

What did Matt take out?

_____

_____

 Often, writers will take out details that do not support the main idea. They will also rewrite sentences for clarity or style. Here is a sample answer:

> Matt took out the phrase the lives of and the sentence What a story she would have to tell geography class.

What other additions or changes did he make?

_____

_____

_____

_____

_____

 Writers will sometimes make changes to use more precise words in their writing. They also look for any problems in spelling or punctuation. Here are the corrections:

> Matt added from a tsunami to sentence 1. He changed funny to bubbly and added a period to the last sentence in paragraph 1. He combined two sentences in paragraph 2 by adding the transition word because. He transposed the words ran and all in the second-to-last sentence. He capitalized as in the last sentence and added deadly in the last sentence.

## Step 5: Publishing

The final step is for Matt to publish his paper. He can do this by using a computer to create his final paper and email it to his teacher. Or, he can handwrite his paper and turn it into his teacher.

# Test Yourself

One of the most destructive tsunamis in history was the Indian Ocean tsunami of December 2004. At about 7:58 a.m. local time on December 26, an earthquake occurred deep under the Indian Ocean, 150 miles off the coast of Sumatra. The huge earthquake measured at least 9.0—one of the biggest ever recorded. The earth shook for eight minutes. Giant sea waves generated by the earthquake reached nine countries.

A tsunami can travel across the ocean at speeds up to 500 miles an hour. Between 15 and 30 minutes after the earthquake, the first tsunami hit Sumatra. The last waves of the tsunami reached Somalia, in Africa, seven hours after the earthquake. In deep ocean water, a tsunami wave may only be a foot higher than the surface of the ocean. When the wave reaches shallow waters near the coasts, it slows down. Then, the top of the wave moves faster than the bottom of the wave, which causes the wave to grow in height. The first wave that hit Thailand reached 30 feet.

Tsunamis are rare in the Indian Ocean. Most people who live in the countries affected by this tsunami had never experienced one. The tsunami came as a complete surprise. About 174,000 people died in the tsunami, and still more were missing.

Immediately after the tsunami, emergency relief efforts began. Food, water, and medical help arrived and shelters were set up for the homeless. Many countries pledged money for economic relief. The cost of relief was estimated to be between four and five billion dollars for the first five years.

One of the great tragedies of the disaster was that many lives could have been saved if a tsunami early warning system had been in place in the Indian Ocean. In the Pacific Ocean, where most tsunamis form, such a system alerts people when earthquakes or other events raise the possibility of a tsunami. Leaders from the Indian Ocean countries and organizations such as the United Nations urgently began to plan for an Indian Ocean warning system after the tsunami. The early warning system became operational in 2006 and will help avert disasters in the future.

Write an essay to explain the causes of the damage done by the tsunami and one useful result of the disaster.

- include a main idea explaining the cause and effect
- use details from the article to support your main idea
- use transition words such as *because, since, so,* and *as a result*

**1** What kind of writing are you being asked to do?

_____

Read
Note
Organize

**2** Who is your audience?

_____

**3** Use the cause and effect chart to plan your writing. Then list ideas from the chart in the order that you will present them in your writing.

Read
Note
**Organize**

| CAUSE | |
|---|---|

| CAUSE | EFFECT |
|---|---|

| CAUSE | |
|---|---|

**4** Use the cause and effect chart and your paragraph plan to help you write your draft. In the first paragraph of your essay, be sure to state the effect. Include the causes in logical order in other paragraphs. Remember to use transitional words and phrases.

_____

_____

_____

_____

_____

_____

_____

_____

_____

_____

_____

_____

_____

_____

_____

_____

_____

_____

_____

_____

_____

_____

**5** Once you have finished your draft, go back over it. Make your revisions on this page. Use the rubric on page 57 to review your writing. Have a peer edit your writing if appropriate.

_____

_____

_____

_____

_____

_____

_____

_____

_____

_____

_____

_____

_____

_____

_____

_____

_____

_____

_____

_____

# RUBRIC for Writing Cause and Effect

## Score 3

- The writing answers all parts of the question.
- There are at least one clear effect and two or three causes.
- The topic sentence in the first paragraph clearly states the most important effect.
- Transition words that are specific to cause and effect connect the ideas.
- The causes are organized in a logical order.
- The writing is easy to read and stays on the subject.
- There are almost no mistakes in grammar, capitalization, punctuation, and spelling.

## Score 2

- The writing answers almost all parts of the question.
- There are at least one generally clear effect and two causes.
- The topic sentence in the first paragraph does not clearly state the most important effect.
- Transition words that are specific to cause and effect connect a few ideas.
- Most of the causes are organized in a logical order.
- The writing is fairly easy to read and mostly stays on the subject.
- There are some mistakes in grammar, capitalization, punctuation, and spelling.

## Score 1

- The writing answers only part of the question.
- The writing is unclear about what the effect and causes are.
- There is no topic sentence in the first paragraph that states the most important effect.
- There are no transition words specific to cause and effect connecting the ideas.
- The causes are not organized in a logical order.
- The writing is not easy to read or is off the subject in many places.
- There are several mistakes in grammar, capitalization, punctuation, and spelling.

**6** When you are satisfied with your writing, you are ready to publish your work. Write your final copy on the lines below.

_____

_____

_____

_____

_____

_____

_____

_____

_____

_____

_____

_____

_____

_____

_____

_____

_____

_____

_____

_____

_____

_____

# Comparison and Contrast

**W.5.1, 2, 4, 5, 8, 9**

Some writing assignments or test questions may ask you to compare and contrast two ideas, events, people, or things. A **comparison** is when you explain how two things are similar, and a **contrast** is when you explain how they are different. There are many ways to structure this type of writing. You might first discuss how two things are alike and then explain how they are different. Or, you may decide to focus on one element and then explain how they are different and how they are the same for the two things being compared and contrasted.

## Guided Practice

**Read the passage. Then answer the questions.**

### from "Climbing Down"

Nikki looked at her watch. They had just one hour of daylight left. Nikki was sure that wasn't enough time to make it safely down the mountain, but Casey disagreed.

"We can do it, Nikki," Casey said in that soft, confident way of hers. Casey never raised her voice. She never even seemed to get tense. Even now, when the girls were lost on Saddleback Mountain, she was calm. She added, "I remember some of these landmarks. I am sure we'll find the trail just beyond those pines."

"No!" Nikki all but shouted. Her voice was full of tension, and she knew she was acting like the younger sister when, after all, she was two years older. She actually surprised herself. She had been hiking since she was 5, and she had developed strong map and compass skills. Still, fear gripped her now. She knew these mountains well enough to know that only a fool would be wandering around on them after dark.

"Look," said Casey, still in the same even tone. "Here's where I think we are on the map. Remember how we went up and down that sharp ridge only about a quarter mile back? I think this is it on the map. At that point my compass read SSE. If we find this streambed," she added, pointing to a depression on the map, "within the next half mile, we'll know we're going the right way. If not, we'll stop then. What do you say?"

Nikki knew Casey, who had been hiking just as long as she had, was good with a map. Up to this point, she had always trusted her with a compass, too. She wanted to give in, but her heart pounded out two beats of fear that spelled no.

Sisters and brothers share many of the same traits, but they are different, too. Nikki and Casey must make a decision together. How will their similarities and their differences help them decide what to do? Write an essay telling what you think they will do and why. In your essay, include details from the story that show:

- the ways the two characters are alike

- ways they are different

- how you decided what you think they will do

## Step 1: Prewriting

Read
**Note**
Organize

Manali underlined important words in the question. What words do you think she underlined?

_____

_____

_____

_____

_____

_____

 Think about what should be included in the essay. Here is a sample answer:

Manali underlined the words <u>Nikki</u> and <u>Casey</u> in sentence 2. She underlined <u>similarities</u> and <u>differences</u> in sentence 3. Then she underlined <u>what you think they will do</u> in sentence 4. In sentence 5, she underlined <u>details from the story</u>. From the question, she knows that her purpose was to write a comparison and contrast and that her audience would be her teacher and classmates.

Next, Manali had to come up with ideas for her essay. What type of graphic organizer do you think she used to plan her writing?

A   web

B   Venn diagram

C   cause and effect chart

D   sequence or time order chart

✓   Choices A, C, and D do not show how two things are the same and how they are different. Choice B is the correct answer. Manali used a Venn diagram. This graphic organizer shows how two things are alike and how they are different. She could have also used a two-column chart.

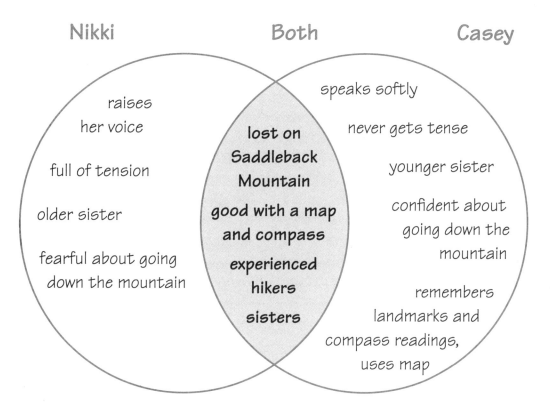

Nikki         Both         Casey

raises her voice

full of tension

older sister

fearful about going down the mountain

**lost on Saddleback Mountain**

**good with a map and compass**

**experienced hikers**

**sisters**

speaks softly

never gets tense

younger sister

confident about going down the mountain

remembers landmarks and compass readings, uses map

The next step is to organize the comparison-contrast writing into paragraphs. Manali organized her writing into three paragraphs. Her first paragraph will show how the characters are alike. The second paragraph will tell how they are different. In the last paragraph, she will tell what she thinks they will do.

# Guided Practice

- Nikki raises her voice, but Casey speaks softly.
- They are lost on Saddleback Mountain.
- They are good with a map and compass.
- Nikki is tense, while Casey stays calm.
- Nikki is fearful about going down the mountain, but Casey is confident.
- They are experienced hikers.
- Nikki is two years older than Casey.
- The girls are sisters.

Which details belong in paragraph 1? Which details belong in paragraph 2?
Write the statements in the correct column.

**Paragraph 1:**

Nikki and Casey are alike.

_____

_____

_____

_____

**Paragraph 2:**

Nikki and Casey are different.

_____

_____

_____

_____

Paragraph 1 explains what Nikki and Casey have in common. Paragraph 2 contrasts the two girls. Here is a sample answer:

| Paragraph 1: | Paragraph 2: |
| --- | --- |
| Nikki and Casey are alike. | Nikki and Casey are different. |
| They are lost on Saddleback Mountain. | Nikki raises her voice, but Casey speaks softly. |
| They are experienced hikers. | Nikki is tense, while Casey stays calm. |
| They are good with a map and compass. | Nikki is two years older than Casey. |
| The girls are sisters. | Nikki is fearful about going down the mountain, but Casey is confident. |

The next step is to write the draft.

# Step 2: Drafting

As sisters, Nikki and Casey are alike. They enjoy the outdoors. They love hiking. As experienced hikers, both of them are good with reading a map. They are also good with using a compass. In this story, however, despite their hiking experience, they are lost on Saddleback mountain.

Nikki and Casey are also different. Nikki is tense. She is afraid of going down the mountain. When she speaks, she raises her voice. And shows her fear. Casey is calm. She seems to be in control of the situation. She's confident about going down the mountain safely. Even though she is the younger sister. She uses the map, her compass and logical thinking to describe the situation. From the passage, you don't find out what happens in the next scene of the story, though.

Even though Nikki is scared, I think they go down the mountain because Casey is confident. And she has a plan. She remembers passing the stream bed marked on they're map. She believes that if they fine it then they know that they're going in the right direction. Nikki will probably follow Casey's lead.

What words did the author use to signal transitions?

_____

_____

_____

✓ Authors use certain words to give clues about what is to come. Transitions help the reader know that there is a change in focus. Certain words let the reader know that two objects are being compared. Other words let the reader know when two things are being contrasted. Here is a sample answer:

*The author used the words alike and both to signal how the two characters are the same. She used the words different and even though to signal a contrast.*

What is the topic sentence in each paragraph?

Paragraph 1: _____

_____

_____

Paragraph 2: _____

Paragraph 3: _____

✓ The topic sentence of a paragraph explains the main idea. The other sentences in the paragraph support the topic sentence, or main idea. Here is a sample answer:

*Paragraph 1: "As sisters, Nikki and Casey are alike." Then the author supports this with details about how the girls are similar. They are sisters. They are both lost. Both are good with a map and compass.*
*Paragraph 2: "Nikki and Casey are also different."*
*Paragraph 3: "Even though Nikki is scared, I think they go down the mountain because Casey is confident."*

**UNIT 1** ▪▪▪▪▪▪▪▪▪▪▪▪▪▪▪▪▪▪▪▪▪▪▪▪▪▪▪▪▪▪▪▪▪▪
Elements of Writing

What details does the author use to support the topic sentence in paragraph 2?

_____

_____

_____

_____

 Think about how the author describes both girls. How do these descriptions support the topic sentence that the girls are different? Here is a sample answer:

The author says that Nikki is tense, nervous, and afraid of going down the mountain. She raises her voice. Nikki is older. The author describes how Casey is different from her sister. Casey is calm, confident, and in control. She uses the map, compass, and logical thinking.

Once the draft is written, the next step is to revise it.

## Step 3: Revising

**Read Manali's revised draft. Then answer the questions.**

As sisters, Nikki and Casey are alike. *in many ways.* They enjoy the outdoors.

They love hiking. As experienced hikers, both of them are good with

reading a map. They are also good *and* with using a compass. In this

story, however, despite their hiking experience, they are lost on

Saddleback mountain.

*In many ways,* Nikki and Casey are also different. Nikki is tense. *In a scene from the story,* She is afraid

of going down the mountain. When she speaks, she raises her voice.

And shows her fear. *In contrast,* Casey is calm. She seems to be in control of the

situation. She's confident about going down the mountain safely.

Even though she is the younger sister. She uses the map, her compass, and logical thinking to describe the situation. ~~From the passage, you don't find out what happens in the next scene of the story, though.~~

Even though Nikki is scared, I think they ^will^ go down the mountain because Casey is confident. ~~And~~ she has a plan. She remembers passing the stream bed marked on they're map. She believes that if they fine it then they know that they're going in the right direction. ^So,^ Nikki will probably follow Casey's lead.

Which sentences did she combine in paragraph 1?

_____

_____

_____

_____

 **Here is a sample answer:**

The author combined the sentence, "As experienced hikers, both of them are good with reading a map" with the sentence, "They are also good with using a compass." The new sentence reads, "As experienced hikers, both of them are good with reading a map and with using a compass."

# Peer Review

Manali used the rubric to review her writing. Then she exchanged papers with another student. They reviewed each other's writing and gave it a score based on the rubric. Then they discussed ways they could each improve their writing.

## RUBRIC for Writing Comparison and Contrast

**Score 3**

- The writing answers all parts of the question.
- There are at least two clear comparisons and two clear contrasts.
- Transitional words and phrases connect the ideas.
- Each paragraph has a topic sentence that clearly states the subject.
- Supporting details are organized in a logical order.
- The writing is easy to read and stays on the subject.
- There are almost no mistakes in grammar, capitalization, punctuation, and spelling.

**Score 2**

- The writing answers almost all parts of the question.
- There are two generally clear comparisons and contrasts.
- Transitional words and phrases connect most ideas.
- A topic sentence stating the subject is missing or unclear.
- Some supporting details are missing or are not in a logical order.
- The writing is fairly easy to read and mostly stays on the subject.
- There are some mistakes in grammar, capitalization, punctuation, and spelling.

**Score 1**

- The writing answers only part of the question.
- There are fewer than two comparisons or two contrasts.
- Very few transitional words and phrases are used to connect ideas.
- More than one topic sentence is missing or unclear.
- Many supporting details are missing or are not in a logical order.
- The writing is not easy to read or is off the subject in many places.
- There are several mistakes in grammar, capitalization, punctuation, and spelling.

The next step is for Manali to edit her writing.

## Step 4: Editing

_____

_____

_____

_____

 Did you find the mistakes? Here is a sample answer:

In paragraph 1, capitalize *mountain*. It should be Saddleback Mountain.

In paragraph 3, make *stream bed* one word. It should be *streambed*.

In paragraph 3, change the contraction *they're* to the pronoun *their*.

In paragraph 3, change the word *fine* to *find*.

## Step 5: Publishing

Once Manali has finished correcting her draft, she is ready to publish it. She could handwrite it on another piece of paper and turn it into her teacher. Or, she could use a word processing program to produce her final copy.

# Test Yourself

## Benjamin Franklin

Benjamin Franklin was born in Boston, Massachusetts, in 1706. He moved to Philadelphia in 1723 to work as a printer. He published a newspaper, *Poor Richard's Almanack,* and his own autobiography. Franklin's talents went well beyond printing and writing, however. He sold books, established a library, and helped organize the first firefighting company in America. Franklin was also a great inventor. He is best remembered for his experiments with electricity, which led to his inventing the lightning rod. He also invented bifocals and a new kind of stove called the Franklin stove. Franklin is also remembered as a patriot and a revolutionary leader. He helped draft the Declaration of Independence, which he signed. He served the new American nation as minister to France and as its first postmaster. He was also a delegate to the Constitutional Convention and helped to make sure that the Constitution was ratified.

## Thomas Jefferson

Born in Virginia in 1743, Thomas Jefferson made the state his lifelong home. A patriot of the American Revolution, Jefferson was a leader in seeking American independence from Great Britain. He was on the committee that drafted the Declaration of Independence and is credited today as its author and one of its most famous signers. He became the governor of Virginia. He also served the new American nation as minister to France. He was still in France when the Constitution was written, but he still worked to make sure it was ratified. In 1796, Jefferson became vice president of the United States. In 1800, he became the nation's third president. One of his great accomplishments in office was the Louisiana Purchase. Jefferson was much more than a patriot and statesman, however. He was also a scientist, a philosopher, and an architect. He designed his own home, Monticello, as well as the University of Virginia, which he helped to found.

Two of the greatest leaders in the early history of our nation were Thomas Jefferson and Benjamin Franklin. Write an essay comparing and contrasting them. Then tell which man you think was more important to America and why you think so.

In your essay, be sure to include details that show:

- ways the two men were alike
- ways they were different
- your reason for choosing who was more important

**1** What is the topic of your essay?

_____

_____

_____

_____

_____

**Read**
**Note**
**Organize**

**2** What kind of writing are you being asked to do?

_____

_____

_____

_____

_____

_____

**3** How will you structure your essay?

_____

_____

_____

_____

_____

_____

**UNIT 1**
Elements of Writing

**4** To plan your essay, use the Venn diagram.

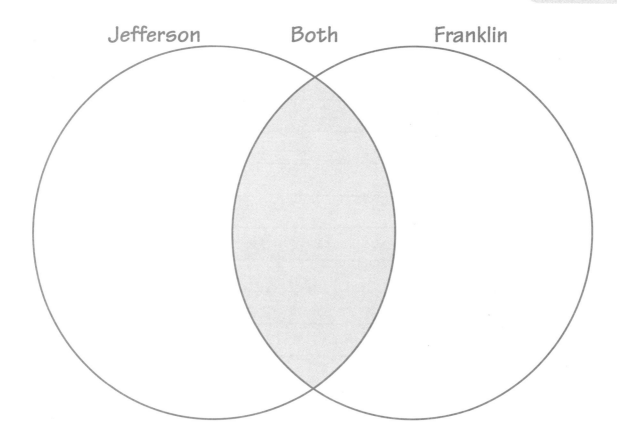

List ideas from your Venn diagram that you will put in each paragraph.

Paragraph 1 _____

_____

_____

Paragraph 2 _____

_____

_____

Paragraph 3 _____

_____

_____

**5** Use your Venn diagram and your paragraph plan to help write your draft. Be sure you begin each paragraph with a topic sentence. Then list your comparisons in paragraph 1 and your contrasts in paragraph 2. Also, remember to use transitional words and phrases. For example, to show comparisons, you can use *and, alike, like, also,* and *in addition.* To show contrast, you can use *but, different, unlike, however,* and *in contrast.*

_____

_____

_____

_____

_____

_____

_____

_____

_____

_____

_____

_____

_____

_____

_____

_____

_____

_____

_____

_____

**UNIT 1**
Elements of Writing

**6** When you have finished your draft, go back over it. Make your revisions on this page. Edit your draft. Use the rubric on page 67 to review your own writing.

_____

_____

_____

_____

_____

_____

_____

_____

_____

_____

_____

_____

_____

_____

_____

_____

_____

_____

_____

_____

_____

_____

**7** Then write your final answer below. Publish your writing by showing it
to your teacher.

_____

_____

_____

_____

_____

_____

_____

_____

_____

_____

_____

_____

_____

_____

_____

_____

_____

_____

_____

_____

_____

_____

_____

_____

# Types of Writing

The steps are the same for all the writing that you do. You want to plan what you will write, then write it, revise and edit it, and finally publish it. However, the types of writing you do will differ. Writing a story or narrative is different than writing a reasoned argument. This unit will review the different types of writing.

- **In Lesson 6,** you will learn how to use facts and opinions to create a reasoned argument. This might be an opinion piece or review. Or, it might be an argument supporting an issue.

- **Lesson 7** focuses on descriptive writing. Writing a good description helps paint a picture of the scene for your readers.

- **In Lesson 8,** you'll learn to write a narrative. A narrative is a story with a beginning, middle, and end.

- **Lesson 9** describes how to write an informational text. This is the type of writing you do for many of your classroom assignments.

# Reasoned Writing

## W.5.1, 4, 5

You need to think about how you use **facts and opinions** when you write. **Facts** can be proved. They can be supported with evidence. **Opinions** are statements that cannot be proved. They are what someone thinks or believes. Some words that can be clues to opinions are: *think, feel, believe, seem.* Words such as *everyone, best, worst, always, never,* and *nobody* also signal opinions. When you write an opinion piece, you need to support your opinion with evidence or facts.

## Guided Practice

Read the article and the information about how one student, Carlos, used the facts from an article about dog parks to write an opinion. Then answer the questions.

### Questions and Answers About Dog Parks

**Q. What is a dog park?**

**A.** A dog park is a place where dogs can run off the leash and play with other dogs. A dog park can be fenced or unfenced. It can be the size of a house lot or many acres. It can be an official place—created just for dogs—or it can be a place where a lot of people have ended up taking their dogs unofficially.

**Q. Why do some people want dog parks?**

**A.** Most towns and cities have leash laws. As a result, most dogs do not get enough exercise. Some of them never have a chance to run free. In some cases, people let their dogs off the leash anyway. These dogs can scare children and do damage to property. Sometimes they even harm people.

**Q. Are all dog parks run by cities and towns?**

**A.** Some dog parks are public places: the town or city government runs them. Some are private. That means a few individuals get together to create a park. In these cases, only some dogs can enter, or people may have to pay a fee for their dog to use the park.

**Q. Why are some people against dog parks?**

**A.** Towns and cities typically have many improvements to make. These may include safe streets, new fire engines, more books for the library, and improvements to the schools. Some people say it is a waste of taxpayer money to build parks for dogs.

**Q. What are the advantages of having a town or city dog park?**

**A.** Pet owners are usually happier. They have a place to meet other dog owners. Sometimes, they get more exercise by taking their pets to the park. Sometimes, people without dogs are happier, too, because people aren't letting their dogs off the leash in the wrong places anymore, such as in children's play areas, sandboxes, and sports fields.

After reading the article, the next step is to read the question carefully.

---

Does your town or city need a dog park? If it already has a dog park, should it have a bigger dog park or more dog parks? Write an article for your neighborhood newsletter that states your opinion for or against a dog park in your town or city.
Be sure to do the following:

- include a topic sentence that clearly states your opinion
- support your opinion with at least three good reasons or facts
- write for adults in your city or town who will take part in making the decision

---

## Step 1: Prewriting

Carlos read the question to make sure that he knew exactly what he was being asked to do. He underlined *article, neighborhood newsletter, opinion for or against,* and *dog park.*

**Read**
Note
Organize

While reading the question, Carlos made notes to help him plan his writing:

Read
**Note**
Organize

    my subject—a dog park in my town
    what I have to write—an article
    my audience—adults who will help decide on the change
    what I have to do—state my opinion and back it up with at least
    three good reasons or facts

The next step is to decide on an opinion and use a graphic organizer to support your opinion. Next, Carlos used a graphic organizer to state his opinion. He also stated some reasons and facts that support it. Here is the organizer Carlos used:

| | |
|---|---|
| **My Opinion:** Bridgewater needs a dog park. | |
| **Reason/Fact 1:** We have a leash law, so dogs can't run free. | |
| **Reason/Fact 2:** They need to get exercise and they need a safe place to play with other dogs. | |
| **Reason/Fact 3:** Some people in our town break the law—they take their dogs to the park and let them off the leash. This scares some young children. | |
| **Reason/Fact 4:** Sometimes the dogs make messes in the park, too. | |
| **Reason/Fact 5:** | |
| **Conclusion:** We need it for the town. | |

What is another fact that Carlos could add to his graphic organizer?

_____

_____

 The owners would also benefit from a dog park. Think about how the owners might benefit. Here is a sample answer:

Dog owners will be happier if we have a dog park. They will have a place to go to meet other dog owners.

After he finished planning what he would write, Carlos was ready to write his draft.

# Step 2: Drafting

The City of Bridgewater should have a dog park. The first reason for this is that we have a leash law. Dogs need exercise, and most of them cant get enough exercise when there on a leash or tied up in a backyard. The perfect place for a dog to run free is a dog park.

Second, we need a special place for dogs to run free a place where they won't bother people. Sometimes, people take their dogs to the park and let them off of the leash. It sometimes scares little kids. I know one little girl on my street that is really, really scared of dogs. Sometimes, the dogs make messes that their owners don't clean up, this ruins parks for people. This is against the law. We need a special place for dogs so people can have clean parks for themselves. And have parks where their children feel safe.

Finally, dog parks are good for people too. At dog parks, dog owners meet other dog owners. They become friends with people who share there own interests. Building a dog park is one way to show that we understand. Building a dog park is for people in our city who have diffrent needs.

Which of these is a transition word Carlos used in his draft?

A   secondly

B   then

C   now

D   finally

> Each of these choices is a transition word. These words give the reader a clue about what is to come. Choice D is the correct answer. This is the only transition word that Carlos used in his draft.

How did Carlos organize his draft? Explain how he organized his opinion piece by identifying the:

Topic Sentence/Opinion:

_____

Fact/Reason 1:

_____

Fact/Reason 2:

_____

Fact/Reason 3:

_____

> In an opinion piece, the author states his opinion and then uses facts and reasons to support it. Here is a sample answer:

Topic Sentence/Opinion:
The City of Bridgewater should have a dog park.
Fact/Reason 1:
We need a place for dogs to get exercise.
Fact/Reason 2:
We need a place where dogs won't bother other people.
Fact/Reason 3:
Dog parks are good for people too.

# Step 3: Revising

The City of Bridgewater should have a dog park. The first reason for this is that we have a leash law, in our city, so dogs cannot run free. Dogs need exercise, and most of them can't get enough exercise when they're [there] on a leash or tied up in a backyard. The perfect place for a dog to run free is a dog park with a fence.

Second, we need a special place for dogs to run free a place where they won't bother people. Sometimes, people take their dogs to the park and let them off of the leash. It scares children [little kids]. ~~I know one little girl on my street that is really, really scared of dogs.~~ Sometimes, the dogs make messes that their owners don't clean up. This ruins parks for people. (This is against the law.) We need a special place for dogs so people can have clean parks for themselves. ~~And have parks~~ where their children feel safe.

Finally, dog parks are good for people, too. At dog parks, dog owners meet other dog owners. They become friends with people who share there own interests. Building a dog park is one way to show that we understand. ~~Building a dog park is for~~ people in our city ~~who~~ have diffrent [different] needs.

Why did Carlos add the words *with a fence* to the last sentence in paragraph 1?

_____

_____

_____

> ✓ **Think about how a dog park is different than walking a dog on a leash. Here is a sample answer:**

> Carlos added the words *with a fence* because the dogs in the dog park would not be on leashes. Without a fence, the dog park would not solve any problems.

Identify and correct a run-on sentence in paragraph 2.

_____

_____

_____

_____

> ✓ **Do you remember what a run-on sentence is? A run-on sentence is two or more sentences that run together without punctuation. Here is a sample answer:**

> The run-on sentence is, "Second, we need a special place for dogs to run free a place where they won't bother people." The correction should be, "Second, we need a special place for dogs to run free. It should be a place where they won't bother people."

**UNIT 2** ▓▓▓▓▓▓▓▓▓▓▓▓▓▓▓▓▓▓▓▓▓▓▓▓▓▓▓▓▓▓▓▓
Types of Writing

# Peer Review

Carlos used this rubric to review his writing. Then he exchanged papers with another student. They reviewed each other's writing and gave it a score based on the rubric. Then they discussed ways they could improve their writing.

Once Carlos has revised his paper and is satisfied with it, his next step is to edit his paper.

## RUBRIC for Reasoned Writing

**Score 3**
- The writing answers all parts of the question.
- The ideas are clear, and appropriate transitions connect them.
- Each paragraph has a topic sentence that clearly states the subject.
- Facts and reasons are clear and are in a logical order.
- The writing is easy to read and stays on the subject.
- Words are used correctly and well.
- There are almost no mistakes in grammar, capitalization, punctuation, and spelling.

**Score 2**
- The writing answers almost all parts of the question.
- The ideas are mostly clear, and transitions connect most of them.
- A topic sentence stating the subject is missing or unclear.
- Some facts and reasons are unclear or are not in a logical order.
- The writing is fairly easy to read and mostly stays on the subject.
- Some words are misused.
- There are some mistakes in grammar, capitalization, punctuation, and spelling.

**Score 1**
- The writing answers only part of the question.
- The ideas are not clear, or they are not connected.
- A topic sentence stating the subject is missing or unclear.
- Most of the facts and reasons are unclear or are not in a logical order.
- The writing is not easy to read or is off the subject in many places.
- Many words are overused or misused.
- There are several mistakes in grammar, capitalization, punctuation, and spelling.

# Step 4: Editing

Identify and correct three more mistakes in Carlos's paper.

_____

_____

_____

✓ When editing a paper, look for problems in grammar, spelling, and other standard English conventions. Did you find these errors?

Paragraph 1: *City should be lowercase not capitalized*
Paragraph 2: *Delete a place*
Paragraph 3: *Change there to the pronoun their*

# Step 5: Publishing

Carlos has finished writing his opinion. Now he would like to publish it. One way to publish it is to type it into the computer and print out a copy for his teacher and classmates to read. However, he thinks a dog park would be a good idea and would like more people to read his opinion. More people might agree with him. He hopes that this might encourage the city of Bridgewater to create a dog park.

List some ways that Carlos could publish his opinion using technology.

_____

_____

_____

✓ There are many ways that someone can publish his opinion. Here is a sample answer:

*Carlos could post his opinion on the city website. He could email it to the editor of the city newsletter or newspaper and ask them to publish it.*

## A Difference Over Goals

**Shawsville, IN 6/24/05** The people of Shawsville are divided over the issue of land.

In the past two weeks, signs have gone up all over town. Some say things like "More Soccer Fields for Shawsville!" and "We Just Want to Play Soccer." Others say "Let's Save Our Land" and "No More Soccer Fields."

People on both sides get a bit excited when you ask them their opinion. This small town has more than 900 children who play soccer, yet it has only three fields. Two of them are at the regional high school and, therefore, sometimes in use by the high school team.

Soccer moms and dads are angry that their children can't play every Saturday and often can't practice more than once a week. They propose building two new fields on the Greenway Conservation Land. They point to a flat meadow that is not far from the parking area. They say it could easily be turned into much needed fields. "Then the children will be happy," they say. They add that playing soccer is excellent exercise and helps their children stay fit.

Some people in Shawsville see the issue very differently, however. "That's conservation land!" they say. They quickly add, "Using that land is against the law!"

They are correct: the town of Shawsville will need, among other legal requirements, to have a special two-thirds vote to use the land. Then there's the cost of building the fields and adding more parking.

The town budget is already strained from last year's addition to the police station. Some people say Shawsville can't afford the project and won't be able to maintain it. Others say that if money is going to be spent, it should be spent adding a classroom to the overcrowded elementary school.

More and more children are playing soccer, lacrosse, baseball, and other sports. Many communities do not have enough sports fields. Imagine that your town or city does not have enough playing fields for all the children who want to play sports. Should your community build a new field? If so, will it be a problem to find the land? Write an article that states your opinion for or against a new sports field.

Be sure to do the following:

- include a topic sentence that clearly states your opinion
- support your opinion with at least three good reasons or facts
- write for your local newspaper, which will be read by many members of your community

**1** What structure will you use for your writing?

Read

Note

**Organize**

_____

_____

_____

_____

_____

**2** How will you publish your writing?

_____

_____

_____

_____

_____

**UNIT 2**
Types of Writing

**3** Fill in the opinion and reasons/facts organizer to plan your article.

| My Opinion: |
| --- |
| Reason/Fact 1: |
| |
| |
| |
| |
| |

4   Now use the organizer to write your draft. Begin each paragraph
    with a topic sentence. Then state and explain each fact or reason.
    Remember to link your ideas with transitions.

_____

_____

_____

_____

_____

_____

_____

_____

_____

_____

_____

_____

_____

_____

_____

_____

_____

_____

_____

_____

_____

_____

_____

_____

**5** When you have finished your draft, go back over it. Make your revisions on this page. Then edit your draft. Use the rubric on page 83 to review your writing. Have a peer edit your writing if appropriate.

**6** When you are satisfied with your writing, you are ready to publish your work. Write your final copy on the lines below. Then show it to your teacher.

_____

_____

_____

_____

_____

_____

_____

_____

_____

_____

_____

_____

_____

_____

_____

_____

_____

_____

_____

_____

_____

_____

# Descriptive Writing

W.5.2, 4–6, 8, 9

Sometimes in your writing you are asked to create a vivid picture of a person, place, or thing. This type of writing is called **descriptive writing.** When writing a description, you first need to decide on the feeling you want your readers to have. Then you choose details that make this feeling come alive.

Using details that relate to the senses is the best way to "paint a picture" of something for the reader. A descriptive paragraph about an early morning walk along the beach might include details about the smell of the ocean, the sight of the blue water and white sand, and the sound of the birds overhead. The details you would choose to describe a walk on a crowded beach in the middle of the afternoon would "paint" quite a different picture of the beach in the reader's mind than the one of the beach early in the morning.

## Guided Practice

**Read the question. Then write a response.**

You have been asked to write a paragraph for younger students about one of your favorite places. Bring this place to life using details about what it looks like, sounds like, smells like, and feels like. Be sure to:

- use details that make the reader feel like he or she is there
- arrange your details in logical order

## Step 1: Prewriting

What words give you clues about what you will be writing?

Read
Note
Organize

_____

_____

_____

Think about the picture you want to give the reader. Also, look for clues that tell you the purpose, audience, and type of writing. Here is a sample answer:

*The words using details about what it looks like, sounds like, smells like, and feels like give clues that the assignment is to write a description. The words a favorite place tell the subject.*

The next step is planning the paragraph.

What type of graphic organizer would you use to plan the paragraph and what would you include?

Read
Note
**Organize**

A   web

B   timeline

C   Venn diagram

D   cause and effect chart

Choice A is the correct answer. A web lets you include details or descriptions. A timeline is best for a narrative. The Venn diagram compares and contrasts two objects. A cause and effect chart shows relationships between what happened and why it happened. Choices B, C, and D are incorrect.

You could use a web or a chart. One student, Nadine, used a sensory chart to plan her paragraph.

| Subject: On the Roof |
| --- |
| **Sight**<br>people and cars below |
| **Sound**<br>dogs barking, the hum of traffic below |
| **Smell**<br>air smells clean up this high |
| **Taste** |
| **Touch/Feel**<br>it's cool out and I shiver |
| **Thoughts/Feelings**<br>feels like a special treat |

# Guided Practice

The smell of blueberry waffles wafted through the air.

   **A**  sight

   **B**  smell

   **C**  sound

   **D**  touch

> Choice B is the correct answer. This detail is about the sense of smell. Choices A, C, and D are incorrect.

I felt very nervous as I walked toward the door.

   **A**  sound

   **B**  feeling

   **C**  touch

   **D**  smell

> This detail explains the nervous feeling that someone had as he walked toward a door. Choice B is the correct answer. Choices A, C, and D are incorrect.

The smooth fabric reminded me of silk.

   **A**  smell

   **B**  feeling

   **C**  sound

   **D**  touch

> This sentence is about the sense of touch. The fabric is smooth like silk. The correct answer is choice D. Choices A, B, and C are incorrect.

Once you've developed a plan, then you can write your draft. Here is what one student, Nadine, wrote. She used her sensory chart to help.

## Step 2: Drafting

**Read the draft below. Then answer the questions.**

From the roof top garden of my apartment building, I watch the people and Cars below and feel like nothing can be wrong with the World. there is always wind here on the roof. Today it's coool out and shiver as it blows against back. The air smells clean up this high. I see a fly by and look at me—maybe wondering if we are sharng the same feeling. i'm amzed at brightly the sun light reflects of the cars passing by. i hear dog barking, and the hum of trafic below. it feels like a special treat to sit so peacefully and so high above the busy street below. The air smells clean up this high.

What specific event was Nadine describing?

_____

_____

 Think about the descriptions that Nadine includes in her draft and how they are related. Here's a sample answer:

Nadine was describing a visit to the rooftop garden on her apartment building.

What words does the writer use to describe the sights she sees?

_____

_____

> ✓ **Writers often use words that describe what they see to help the reader understand what the writer is trying to convey. Here is a sample answer:**

people and cars below; sunlight
_____

What words does she use to describe touch?

_____

_____

> ✓ **Touch is another sensory detail that helps set a mood or scene. Here is a sample answer:**

wind, cool
_____

Once you've gotten your thoughts and ideas written into a draft, the next steps are to revise and edit the draft.

## Step 3: Revising

(Title)

From the roof top garden of my apartment building, I watch the

the
people and Cars below and feel like nothing can be wrong with the

World. there is always wind here on the roof. Today it's coool out, and

the wind        my
shiver as it blows against back. The air smells clean up this high. I

bird
see a fly by and look at me—maybe wondering if we are sharng the

a    how
same feeling. i'm amzed at brightly the sun light reflects of the cars

a                     f
passing by. i hear dog barking, and the hum of trafic below. it feels

like a special treat to sit so peacefully ~~and so high~~ above the busy

street below. ~~The air smells clean up this high~~

Why has the word *it* been replaced with *the wind* in sentence 3?

_____

_____

 *It* is a pronoun. *The wind* is a noun. Here is a sample answer:

The change makes it clear what Nadine is describing. She is
describing the wind and how it touches her back.

Why did Nadine cross out the last sentence?

_____

_____

 **The conclusion should sum up the overall feeling of the subject. Do you think the last sentence does this? Here is a sample answer:**

> Nadine crossed out the last sentence because it is a detail. It is not a concluding statement. Also, this sentence appeared in sentence 4 of the paragraph. It is a repetition.

Write a title for this descriptive paragraph.

_____

_____

 **Using a title helps the reader understand what they will be reading. Here is a sample answer:**

> One title that might be used is "My Rooftop Garden."

# Peer Review

Nadine used this rubric to review her writing. Then she exchanged papers with another student. They reviewed each other's writing and gave it a score based on the rubric. Then they discussed ways they could improve their writing.

## Rubric for Descriptive Writing

**Score 3**
- The writing answers all parts of the question.
- The supporting details appeal to the senses and draw the reader in.
- The introduction, supporting details, and concluding sentence are clear.
- The concluding sentence sums up the overall feeling of the paragraph.
- Words are used correctly and well.
- There are almost no mistakes in grammar, capitalization, punctuation, and spelling.

**Score 2**
- The writing answers almost all parts of the question.
- Some of the supporting details appeal to the senses and draw the reader in.
- The introduction, supporting details, and concluding sentences are somewhat unclear.
- The concluding sentence relates to the paragraph.
- Some worlds are misused.
- There are some mistakes in grammar, capitalization, punctuation, and spelling.

**Score 1**
- The writing answers only part of the question.
- The supporting details do not appeal to the senses or draw the reader in.
- The introduction, supporting details, and concluding sentences are not easy to identify.
- The concluding sentence does not relate to the paragraph.
- Many words are overused or misused.
- There are several mistakes in grammar, capitalization, punctuation, and spelling.

Once Nadine has revised her paper and is satisfied with it, her next step is to edit her paper.

**UNIT 2**
Types of Writing

# Step 4: Editing

Reread Nadine's revised draft on page 96. Then find and correct six more errors.

_____

_____

_____

_____

_____

_____

✓ Did you find all the errors? Here is a sample answer:

Change *World* to lowercased *world* in sentence 1.

Delete the extra letter *O* in *coool* in sentence 3.

Change *i'm* to *I'm* in sentence 6.

Make *sun light* one word in sentence 6.

Change *of* to *off* in sentence 6.

Change the lowercase *i* to a capital *I* in sentence 7.

# Step 5: Publishing

The last step is to publish her paper. Nadine can do this by reading it to the class, if her teacher allows her to do so. Or, she can turn it into her teacher.

# Test Yourself

Mrs. Arnold has put together a list for Thanksgiving dinner. She'll be cooking for her family.

## Thanksgiving Shopping List

| | |
|---|---|
| 18-lb turkey | carrots |
| 2 bags onions | brown sugar |
| 3 packages mushrooms | 5 lemons |
| fresh cranberries | 4 pie crusts |
| 8 sticks butter | pecans (for pie) |
| bread for stuffing | apples (for pie) |
| 1 lb green beans | 3 cans pumpkin filling (for pie) |
| 6 sweet potatoes | ice cream (chocolate, vanilla, |
| 2 butternut squashes | strawberry) |
| yeast for dough | whipping cream |
| lettuce | chocolate topping |
| tomatoes | coffee |
| cucumbers | cinnamon |

Think of a real or imaginary Thanksgiving dinner. Use items from Mrs. Arnold's shopping list to write a description telling the details of this Thanksgiving meal. What was served? How did the food smell and taste?

- Describe the details of the meal using words related to the five senses.
- Make sure your conclusion sums up the overall feeling of your description.

**1** What kind of writing are you being asked to do, and how do you know?

_____

_____

_____

_____

_____

**2** What subject are you being asked to write about?

_____

_____

_____

_____

_____

**3** Reread the list of items and the question. Then write a descriptive paragraph about a real or imaginary dinner. Use the sensory chart to help you plan your writing.

| Subject: |
| --- |
| Sight |
| Sound |
| Smell |
| Taste |
| Touch/Feel |
| Thoughts/Feelings |

**4** Write a draft. Before you begin, review the graphic organizer. Think about how the topic sentence will introduce the subject and the details that follow. How will supporting details make readers feel like they are there? Make sure to use interesting and lively words.

_____

_____

_____

_____

_____

_____

_____

_____

_____

_____

_____

_____

_____

_____

_____

_____

_____

_____

_____

_____

_____

_____

**5** When you have finished you draft, go back over it. Make your
revisions below. Then edit the draft. Use the rubric on page 98 to
review the paper. Have a peer edit your paper if appropriate.

_____

_____

_____

_____

_____

_____

_____

_____

_____

_____

_____

_____

_____

_____

_____

_____

_____

_____

_____

_____

_____

**6** Write your final description on this page. Publish your writing by showing it to your teacher.

_____

_____

_____

_____

_____

_____

_____

_____

_____

_____

_____

_____

_____

_____

_____

_____

_____

_____

_____

_____

_____

_____

_____

# Narrative Writing

**W.5.3–6**

**Narrative writing** tells a story with a beginning, middle, and end. A narrative can be a made-up story or it can be based on real events. A **personal narrative** is based on events that happened to the writer over a short period of time. A personal narrative might be about the first time you were frightened or the first time you went on a trip. When you write a personal narrative, you use the pronouns *I* and *me*.

A story that is made up is a **creative narrative.** Novels and short stories are creative narratives. A writer might make up the plot but many times they use details and information from real life to make their stories realistic or believable.

## Guided Practice

**Read the question. Then answer the questions.**

> Write a story for your class about a time you had to go to the doctor.
> - Choose one specific visit when something interesting happened.
> - Arrange your details in time order.
> - Use dialogue in your story.
> - Be sure to include clues to the setting.
> - Write three paragraphs.

## Step 1: Prewriting

Read the question carefully. What words give clues about what you are being asked to write?

**Read
Note
Organize**

_____

_____

_____

_____

Here is a sample answer:

> The word *story* tells that you will be writing a narrative. *Clues to the setting* means that you will need to tell readers when and where the story happened. *Choose one specific visit* tells that the assignment is about one event. *Arrange your details in time order* lets you know that the events should be told in the order in which they happened.

What is the setting?

_____

_____

_____

 Think about where a story takes place. Here's a sample answer:

> The setting is the particular time and place in which the narrative takes place. The time might be "yesterday" or "once upon a time." The place might be outer space or at school.

What is dialogue?

_____

 Think about the stories you have read. How do the characters communicate their thoughts and feelings to each other? Here is a sample answer:

> Dialogue is the words that the characters speak.

**UNIT 2** ▓▓▓▓▓▓▓▓▓▓▓▓▓▓▓▓▓▓▓▓▓▓▓▓▓▓▓▓▓▓▓▓▓▓▓▓▓▓▓▓▓▓▓▓▓▓
Types of Writing

A graphic organizer helps you plan what you are going to write. One student, Tasha, used this graphic organizer to write a story about one time she went to the doctor.

| Subject: My Last Visit to Doctor Smith's Office |
| --- |
| Time Order (Chronological Order) |
| 1. Nipper got out of the backyard; broke my pinky while chasing after him |
| 2. scared on the way to Dr. Smith's; I was sad about losing Nipper |
| 3. |
| 4. |
| 5. |
| 6. |
| 7. |

Look at the items below and the numbered boxes in the graphic organizer. Number the items below in the order in which you think they happened.

_____ I heard a strange yelping sound at Dr. Smith's.

_____ Nipper was there!

_____ I wanted to get up and investigate the room the sound was coming from, but Mom wouldn't let me.

_____ I ran across the office toward the sound.

_____ I hugged Nipper as Dr. Smith put a splint on my pinky.

✓ **Think about what happened first, second, and last. Did you put them in the correct order? Here is the correct answer:**

\_\_\_3\_\_ I heard a strange yelping sound at Dr. Smith's.

\_\_\_6\_\_ Nipper was there!

\_\_\_4\_\_ I wanted to get up and investigate the room the sound was coming from, but Mom wouldn't let me.

\_\_\_5\_\_ I ran across the office toward the sound.

\_\_\_7\_\_ I hugged Nipper as Dr. Smith put a splint on my pinky.

# Step 2: Drafting

My last visit to the doctor's office hapened when I broke my finger, while chasing after Nipper. Nipper was my pupy, and she had gotten out of the backyard that morning. Her paw was hurt. I had no idea that my visit to Dr. Smith's office would be such an interesting one.

On the way to Dr. Smith's office, I was feeling scared because I didn't know what was going to hapen to my finger. I was also very sad about losing Nipper that morning. We were all sad about losing little Nipper. He was such a special member of our family.

When my mother and me walked into the doctor's office. I heard a yelping sound, like a howling. The sound made me forget about my finger. All I wanted to do was to get up and check out the room from which the sound was coming. "Sit quietly and wait for the doctor, Tasha," my mom said. "I can't," I said, getting up. The yelping was loud, so I ran. Across the office toward the sound. There was nipper! "Nipper!" I cried. A man had brought her to Dr. Smith's because he had found her near by. I through my arms around Nipper and sat beside her. As Dr. Smith put a splint on my finger. I had not idea that my visit to Dr. Smith's office would end up reuniting me with Nipper!

What specific event does Tasha focus on?

_____

_____

In a personal narrative, the focus is on an event that happened during a short time period. Here is a sample answer:

Tasha focused on a time when she was reunited with her lost puppy.

What words or phrases does she use to show time order?

_____

Time order or chronological order is the order in which events occur. There are specific words that can signal time order. Here is a sample answer:

last visit, that morning, on the way, that morning, when my mother and me walked into

What dialogue does she use?

_____

_____

_____

_____

Dialogue is the words that the characters speak. Here is a sample answer:

Tasha calls out her dog's name when she sees him. "Nipper!" Her mother tells her to sit quietly. "Sit quietly and wait for the doctor, Tasha," my mom said. Tasha tells her that she can't sit. "I can't," I said, getting up.

When you are finished writing your draft, the next step is to revise it.

## Step 3: Revising

My last visit to the doctor's office hapened when I broke my finger while chasing after Nipper. Nipper was my pupy, and she had gotten out of the backyard that morning. Her paw was hurt. I had no idea that my visit to Dr. Smith's office would be such an interesting one.

On the way to Dr. Smith's office, I was feeling scared because I didn't know what was going to hapen to my finger. I was also very sad about losing Nipper that morning. We were all sad about losing little Nipper. She was such a special member of our family.

When my mother and me walked into the doctor's office, I heard a yelping sound, like a dog howling. The strange sound made me forget about my finger. All I wanted to do was to get up and check out the room from which the sound was coming. "Sit quietly and wait for the doctor, Tasha," my mom said. "I can't," I said, getting up. The yelping was loud, so I ran. Across the office toward the sound. There was nipper! "Nipper!" I cried. A man had brought her to Dr. Smith's because he had found her near by. I threw my arms around Nipper and sat beside her. As Dr. Smith put a splint on my finger. I had not idea that my visit to Dr. Smith's office would end up reuniting me with Nipper!

What did Tasha do to revise the structure of her draft?

_____

**Each paragraph talks about an event. Here is a sample answer:**

*She created a fourth paragraph beginning with A man had brought…*

**UNIT 2**
Types of Writing

# Peer Review

The next step once you have revised your draft is to make sure the paper is free of errors. Tasha used this rubric to review her writing. Then she exchanged papers with another student. They reviewed each other's writing and gave it a score based on the rubric. Then they discussed ways they could improve their writing.

## Rubric for Writing a Narrative

**Score 3**
- The writing answers all parts of the question.
- The supporting details are in time order and relate directly to the main topic.
- The setting is clearly suggested.
- The concluding sentences sum up the preceding paragraphs and bring them to a close.
- Words are used correctly and well.
- There are almost no mistakes in grammar, capitalization, punctuation, and spelling.

**Score 2**
- The writing answers almost all parts of the question.
- At least a few supporting details relate directly to the main topic and are in time order.
- The setting is not clear.
- The concluding sentences relate to the preceding paragraphs.
- Some words are misused.
- There are some mistakes in grammar, capitalization, punctuation, and spelling.

**Score 1**
- The writing answers only part of the question.
- The supporting details do not relate directly to a main topic and are not in time order.
- The writer doesn't include a setting.
- The concluding sentences do not relate to the preceding paragraphs.
- Many words are overused or misused.
- There are several mistakes in grammar, capitalization, punctuation, and spelling.

Once Tasha has revised her paper and is satisfied with it, her next step is to edit her paper.

## Step 4: Editing

Read the revised draft on page 110. Then answer the questions.

Why did Tasha change *He* to *She?*

_____

> Make sure that your pronouns agree with the subject. Here is a sample answer:

*She changed He to She because Nipper was a female.*

Why did Tasha change *through* to *threw?*

_____

_____

> Sometimes a word has two spellings and two meanings although both words sound alike. Here is a sample answer:

*Through should be threw because the word describes the action of throwing her arms around the dog.*

**UNIT 2** ▨▨▨▨▨▨▨▨▨▨▨▨▨▨▨▨▨▨▨▨▨▨▨▨▨▨▨▨
Types of Writing

Look for five more errors. Then explain the corrections.

_____

_____

_____

_____

_____

✓ **Did you find all the errors? Here is a sample answer:**

Correction 1: add a second p to hapened in paragraph 1
Correction 2: add a second p to hapen in paragraph 2
Correction 3: change my mother and me to my mother and I
Correction 4: delete the period after ran, and lowercase across
Correction 5: capitalize the dog's name nipper

## Step 5: Publish

When you are satisfied with what you have written, you are ready to publish it. If you are doing an assignment for class, you can either handwrite the paper or use a computer. If it is a test, you will need to handwrite it. Make sure that your handwriting is clear.

# Test Yourself

## On Your Marks, Get Set, Go!
## Smith and Jones Lead the Eagles to Victory

Yesterday's girls' track meet brought the Eagles an unexpected victory over the Lions in the 400-meter relay category.

The rain poured down on the starting line as the runners, including Jennifer Smith of the Eagles and Maria Gonzalez of the Lions, listened hard for the sound of the gun. Bang! They were off! For an instant, Smith was in the lead. A second later, there was Gonzalez, inching closer. Smith, clearly running at full speed, looked pained as Gonzalez suddenly sped ahead. Time seemed to slow down as Gonzalez reached out to pass the baton to her teammate, Donna Chow. The stands were silent as Gonzalez's baton grazed Chow's hand and dropped to the ground! Smith, only a second behind, successfully passed her baton on to Jones—one of the Eagles' fastest runners. There was no catching up for the Lions, and the Eagles soared to victory!

1  What specific event is this narrative writing focused on?

_____

_____

_____

_____

_____

Read
Note
Organize

**2** What are some of the details and words that bring this story to life for readers?

_____

_____

_____

_____

_____

**Read the article again. Then answer the question.**

> Imagine that you were at the race. Write a narrative about the race based on the article. Write a personal narrative as if you were in the race or were an onlooker. In your narrative, be sure to include:
> - a plot or story told in time order
> - details that make the story realistic, including dialogue
> - a sense of the setting
>
> Use the chart to help answer the question and to arrange the narrative's events in time order.

**3** What kind of writing are you being asked to do, and how do you know?

Read
Note
Organize

_____

_____

_____

_____

_____

**4** Who is your audience?

_____

_____

_____

_____

_____

**5** Fill in the chart to help you answer the test question and to arrange
the events in time order.

| Subject: | | |
|---|---|---|
| **Time Order** (Chronological Order) | | |
| 1. | | |
| 2. | | |
| 3. | | |
| 4. | | |
| 5. | | |
| 6. | | |

**UNIT 2**
Types of Writing

**6** Write your draft. Before you begin, review your graphic organizer. Think about the main subject of your paragraphs. Is it specific enough? Are the supporting details listed in time order? Did you include dialogue? Remember to use words that bring your story to life and make readers want to know what happens next.

_____

_____

_____

_____

_____

_____

_____

_____

_____

_____

_____

_____

_____

_____

_____

_____

_____

_____

_____

_____

_____

**7** When you have finished your draft, go back over it. Make your revisions on this page. Edit your draft. Use the rubric on page 111 to review your paper. Have a peer edit it if appropriate.

_____

_____

_____

_____

_____

_____

_____

_____

_____

_____

_____

_____

_____

_____

_____

_____

_____

_____

_____

_____

_____

_____

_____

_____

**8** Write your final answer on the lines below. Publish your writing by showing it to your teacher.

_____

_____

_____

_____

_____

_____

_____

_____

_____

_____

_____

_____

_____

_____

_____

_____

_____

_____

_____

_____

_____

# Informational Writing

**W.5.2, 4–6, 8, 9**

Informational writing is the type of writing you do most often. This is the type of writing you do when you write a report or answer a question on a test. Informational writing is factual. It should be clear and direct.

Informational writing can be structured in different ways. However, the reader should be able to clearly follow what is being said. Cause and effect, main idea and detail, comparison and contrast, or sequence are different structures used for informational writing. The structure used is often determined by the purpose or content.

## Guided Practice

**Read the assignment. Then answer the questions.**

> Write directions for younger students explaining how to use the computer to find information for a project. Write a paper with the directions you will give for searching the Web.
>
> - Be sure to put the steps in order and include all the steps that you usually follow.
> - Write two or more paragraphs.
> - Explain any terms with which you think readers will not be familiar.

## Step 1: Prewriting

Here's how one student, Daniel, approached the assignment. He reread the assignment, and then underlined key words about the purpose and structure of the assignment.

**Read**
**Note**
Organize

What important words do you think he underlined? What did they tell him?

_____

_____

_____

For most assignments and questions, you want to know the audience, the main purpose, the length, and the format or structure. Here is a sample answer:

Daniel probably underlined <u>directions.</u> This tells him that he is explaining a process. He also underlined <u>steps</u> and <u>order.</u> He knows that a sequence of steps is the best way to structure his writing. Daniel probably underlined <u>younger students.</u> This tells him his audience. Knowing his audience helps him know what tone and style to use. The phrase <u>two or more paragraphs</u> tells the length.

The next step is to make a writing plan. Daniel chose to use a sequence chart to plan his writing.

Read
Note
**Organize**

| Looking up Information on the Web | |
|---|---|
| Step 1 | First, choose a topic that you would like to learn more about. |
| Step 2 | Next, using your computer, choose a search engine that will help you find websites about your topic. If you need help, you can ask a teacher or a librarian. |
| Step 3 | Then, pick some key words about your topic. |
| Step 4 | |
| Step 5 | |
| Step 6 | |

Look at the items below. Then choose three to complete the sequence chart. Label the choices Step 4, Step 5, and Step 6 in that order.

_____ Finally, choose a website that you want to read more about and click on it.

_____ Next, type your key words into the search engine and press the return key.

_____ Write out all of the results you do not want on a separate sheet of paper.

_____ After you press the return key, you will see a list of websites about your topic.

_____ Ask the librarian to help you turn on the computer.

Understanding the order in which tasks must be accomplished is important when writing directions. If tasks are not completed in the proper sequence, then the process will not work. Here is a sample answer:

Step 4  Next, type your key words into the search engine and press the return key.

Step 5  After you press the return key, you will see a list of websites about your topic.

Step 6  Finally, choose a website that you want to read more about and click on it.

## Step 2: Drafting

**Read the draft. Then answer the questions.**

Looking up information on the Web can sem confusing at first. . . sometimes it's hard to know where to begin. Here are some basic steps can follow to find the information you're looking for. Don't forget to make sure you have a good electrical connection.

First, choose a topic that you would like to learn more about. I like water and stars as topics. Next, using your computer, choose a search engine that will help find websites about your topic. If need help, you can ask a teacher or librarian. Then, pick some key words about your topic. Try to be as specific as you can. Next, type your key words into the search engine and the return key. Next, type your key words into the search engine and the return key. After you press the return key, you will see a list of wesites about your topic. Finally, chose a website that you want to read more about and click on it. These basic steps will help you more easily locate the information you're looking for on the Web.

**UNIT 2** ▰▰▰▰▰▰▰▰▰▰▰▰▰▰▰▰▰▰▰▰▰▰▰▰▰▰▰▰▰▰
Types of Writing

How did Daniel organize his directions?

_____

_____

Informational writing can be organized in different ways depending on the content. Here is a sample answer:

The directions are written in the order in which a student would do each task.

What transitional words did Daniel use?

_____

_____

Transitional words help alert the reader to what is happening. Here is a sample answer:

Daniel used transitional words that gave clues about what should happen in what order. He used words such as *First, Next, Then, After,* and *Finally.*

# Step 3: Revising

Looking up information on the Web can sem confusing at first. 𝓁 sometimes it's hard to know where to begin. Here are some basic steps can follow to find the information you're looking for. ~~Don't forget to make sure you have a good electrical connection.~~

First, choose a topic that you would like to learn more about. ~~I like water and stars as topics.~~ Next, using your computer, choose a search engine that will help <sup>you</sup> find websites about your topic. If <sup>you</sup> need help, you can ask a teacher or librarian. Then, pick some key words about your topic. Try to be as specific as you can. Next, type your key words into the search engine and <sup>press</sup> the return key. Next, type your key words into the search engine and the return key. After you press the return key, you will see a list of wesites about your topic. Finally, chose a website that you want to read more about and click on it. These basic steps will help you more easily locate the information you're looking for on the Web.

Why was the second sentence in paragraph 2 deleted?

    A   It was out of order.

    B   It was the main idea.

    C   It repeated another sentence.

    D   It did not provide useful information.

**Distinguishing between important and unimportant sentences is essential for good writing. The second sentence is not the main idea. It is not out of order. The sentence is not a repetition of another sentence. Choices A, B, and C are incorrect. This sentence is an opinion. It does not provide useful information for searching the Web. Choice D is the correct answer.**

Why does Daniel's last sentence work well as a concluding sentence?

_____

_____

**The concluding sentence has a strong relationship to the main idea of a text. Here is a sample answer:**

Daniel's last sentence sums up the main idea of his draft.

# Peer Review

Daniel used this rubric to review his writing. Then he exchanged papers with another student. They reviewed each other's writing and gave it a score based on the rubric. Then they discussed ways they could improve their writing.

## Rubric for Informational Writing

**Score 3**

- The writing answers all parts of the question.
- The ideas are well developed and organized in a way that makes sense.
- There is a clear main idea and details to support it.
- The writing is easy to read and holds the reader's attention.
- Words are used correctly and well.
- There are almost no mistakes in grammar, capitalization, punctuation, and spelling.

**Score 2**

- The writing answers almost all parts of the question.
- At least a few ideas are well developed and connected to one another.
- There is a main idea and some details to support it, though they may be somewhat unclear.
- The writing mostly stays on the subject but may have some details that don't belong.
- Some words may be misused.
- There are some mistakes in grammar, capitalization, punctuation, and spelling.

**Score 1**

- The writing answers only part of the question.
- The ideas don't go together well and they are not organized in a way that makes sense.
- The main idea is unclear, or there may be several main ideas.
- The writing strays from the main subject and is hard to follow.
- Many words are overused or misused.
- There are several mistakes in grammar, capitalization, punctuation, and spelling.

Once Daniel has revised his paper and is satisfied with it, his next step is to edit his paper.

**UNIT 2**
Types of Writing

## Step 4: Editing

_____

_____

_____

_____

_____

When you edit a draft, look for misspelled words, words that are missing, repetitions of words or sentences, and that standard language conventions are followed. Here is a sample answer:

Correction 1: In the first sentence of paragraph 1, change *sem* to *seem*.

Correction 2: In sentence 3 of paragraph 1, add the word *you* between the words *steps* and *can*.

Correction 3: In paragraph 2, delete the sentence "Next, type your key words into the search engine and the return key." It appears twice.

Correction 4: In sentence 8 of paragraph 2, change *wesites* to *websites*.

Correction 5: In sentence 9 of paragraph 2, change *chose* to *choose*.

## Step 5: Publishing

The last step is to publish his paper. Daniel can do this by reading it to the class, if his teacher allows him to do so. Or, he can turn it into his teacher.

# Test Yourself

**Read the timeline and the question. Then answer the questions.**

## The Life of Dr. Martin Luther King Jr. (MLK)

**1928**

**January 15** MLK is born in Atlanta, GA.

**1935**

**September** MLK begins school at an all black elementary school in Atlanta, GA.

**1944**

**June** MLK enters Morehouse College in Atlanta.

**1948**

**February** MLK is ordained a Baptist minister. He enters the Crozer Theological Seminary in Chester, PA.

**1953**

**June** MLK and Coretta Scott are married.

**1954**

**October** MLK becomes pastor of the Dexter Avenue Church in Montgomery, AL.

**1955**

**June** MLK receives his Ph.D. in theology from Boston University.
**December 1** Mrs. Rosa Parks refuses to give up her bus seat to a white man in Montgomery, AL.
**December 5** MLK leads a year-long boycott of the Montgomery buses.

**1957**

**January** The Southern Christian Leadership Conference is founded. Dr. King is chosen president.

**1959**

**February** MLK visits India and studies Mahatma Gandhi's methods of nonviolent protest.

**1960**

**January** MLK becomes co-pastor of the Ebenezer Baptist Church with his father.

**1961**

**May** "Freedom riders" (groups of black and white people who ride buses through the South to challenge segregation) leave Washington, D.C., by bus. The bus is burned by opponents of desegregation, and the riders are beaten upon arrival in Birmingham, AL.

**1963**

**April 12** MLK is arrested and jailed (for the thirteenth time) during a march in Birmingham, AL.
**August 28** 250,000 people demonstrate in Washington, D.C., for civil rights. MLK meets with President Kennedy and delivers his "I Have a Dream" speech.

**1964**

**December** MLK is awarded the Nobel Peace Prize.

**1965**

The 1965 Voting Rights Act, which King sought, is signed by President Johnson.

**1968**

**April 3** MLK delivers his last speech, "I've Been to the Mountaintop."
**April 4** MLK is assassinated in Memphis, TN.

Your teacher has asked you to write a report for the class about the life of Dr. Martin Luther King Jr. Write three or more paragraphs about Dr. King's life based on the timeline.

- Make sure your first paragraph states the main idea of your report.
- Be sure to use transitional words like *first, next,* and *finally* to connect facts and events in the order in which they happened.
- Use the sequence chart to help you write your draft.

**1** Who is your audience?

_____

_____

_____

_____

Read
Note
Organize

**2** Use the sequence chart to help you plan your writing.

The Life of Dr. Martin Luther King Jr.

Step 1

**3** Write your draft. Before you begin, review your graphic organizer. Think about what your main idea should be. What is it that you are going to explain? Are all the facts and events in order? Do you need to add details to explain each step better? Remember to use transitional words such as *first, next, after,* and *finally* to help your sentences flow smoothly.

_____

_____

_____

_____

_____

_____

_____

_____

_____

_____

_____

_____

_____

_____

_____

_____

_____

_____

_____

_____

**4** When you have finished your draft, go back over it. Make your revisions on this page. Edit your draft. Use the rubric on page 126 to review your work. Have a peer edit it if appropriate.

_____

_____

_____

_____

_____

_____

_____

_____

_____

_____

_____

_____

_____

_____

_____

_____

_____

_____

_____

_____

_____

_____

**5** Publish your answer by writing it on this page. Then show it to your teacher.

_____

_____

_____

_____

_____

_____

_____

_____

_____

_____

_____

_____

_____

_____

_____

_____

_____

_____

_____

_____

_____

_____

_____

_____

_____

_____

**UNIT 2** ▓▓▓▓▓▓▓▓▓▓▓▓▓▓▓▓▓▓▓▓▓▓▓▓▓▓▓▓▓▓▓▓▓▓▓▓▓▓▓▓▓
Types of Writing

# Research

Much of the writing you do is shorter assignments or responses to test questions. A research paper is a longer writing assignment that requires good writing skills as well as good research skills. Knowing where to find information and how to organize this information are important skills in writing a research paper. The process for writing the research paper is the same as the writing you've done in the previous lessons. This unit will look at the other skills needed to produce a strong report.

- **Lesson 10** focuses on finding information and taking good research notes. This will help you when you write your research paper.

- **In Lesson 11,** you'll learn how to create a strong thesis statement. You'll also learn how to organize your research and use an outline to create a structure for your writing.

- **Lesson 12** discusses how to write a research paper. The source list is an important part of the research paper. This lesson will help you create a source list.

# Researching Sources and Content

## W.5.2, 4–9

**Research** means using different sources to find out about a subject. If you were researching where the Bengal tiger lives, you would use different sources than you would if you were researching a person's life. These sources can be as different as a letter, a group's website, an encyclopedia, or an interview with an expert. Knowing what sources to use and how to find these sources is a valuable skill.

Writing about your research is a process done in steps. Many of these steps are already familiar to you.

Step 1: Determine the topic.

Step 2: Research the topic by identifying sources of information and taking notes.

Step 3: Determine the thesis statement.

Step 4: Outline the paper to create the structure of the paper.

Step 5: Write the paper.

Step 6: Credit the sources.

## Step 1: Determine the Topic

The first step is deciding on your research topic. Your teacher will give you a general category or subject. Then you will choose a topic. Or, your teacher might assign you a topic. Marco's teacher has given the class an assignment to find out more about a career that interests them. Marco has decided to research and write about the job of engineer.

## Step 2: Research the Topic

Once you know what you will be writing about, then you need to find information about the subject. Sometimes you will be told what sources to use or where to find them. Your teacher might tell you to use both print and web sources. Or, you might be asked to interview someone to find out information. You can find information in newspapers, magazines, books, and on the Internet. A librarian can help you find the materials that you need.

An important part of researching a topic is determining whether the source can be trusted. For example, if you were researching Earth's solar system, you might find Pluto listed as the ninth planet of the solar system in older science books. Newer science materials would not list Pluto as a planet. You would need to decide which is the most reliable source of information. Here are some questions that will help you do this:

- What is the source of the information?
- How old is the information?
- Who wrote the information?
- Why did they write the information?
- Do other sources agree?

## Guided Practice

**Read the passage. Then answer the questions.**

Marco's teacher has assigned the class a research project about careers. He told the students to use at least three sources. They should use both primary and secondary sources. Marco knows that a primary source is a firsthand account. An account by someone who was not there is a secondary source.

Marco has decided on his three sources. He will ask his father about his work as an engineer. This would be a firsthand account. Marco has decided to use the federal government's Occupational Handbook to find out more about the engineering field.

He needs to use a website, too. Marco's teacher has told the class to use only trusted websites. He explained how to use web addresses to tell if a site can be trusted. Government websites end in *.gov*. Universities end in *.edu*. Organizations use *.org*. Business websites end in *.com*.

Which of the following would *not* be the most trusted source about careers in engineering?

A   .gov

B   .edu

C   .com

D   .org

Choice A, B, and D are incorrect. These are considered to be trusted or reliable sources of information. Choice C is the correct answer. Some commercial websites might be good sources of information, but not all of these websites can be trusted.

Which of the following is a primary resource that Marco can use for his paper?

A   book

B   website

C   interview

D   magazine

 A primary source is a firsthand source. An interview with an engineer would be a primary source. Choice C is the correct answer. A book, website, and magazine would be considered a secondhand, or secondary, source. Choices A, B, and D are incorrect.

Why did Marco's teacher tell the class to use at least three sources?

_____

_____

_____

_____

_____

_____

 Different sources may have different purposes. An engineer might give information about what happens during a typical day. An encyclopedia may provide general information about the different types of engineers. Here is a sample answer:

> Marco's teacher wants the class to use a number of sources so they can double-check information. He also wants them to use more than one source so the students can find out as much information as possible about a career. One source might give an engineer's salary. Another source might explain what type of education an engineer needs to do his job.

# Notetaking

Taking notes is an important part of researching. There are many ways to take notes. One of the most common is to use a note card and list the information and the source where you found it.

It's best to use a new note card for every fact. Only write on one side of note card. If you write on the back of the card, use an arrow or the word *over* to remind you that you wrote information on the back of the card.

You can list the source on the card. Or, you can make a list of your resources and number each source on the list. Then put the number of the source on the note card. This will tell you where you found the information. If the source is a book, you should include the title, author, publisher, publication date, and the page number where you found the information. For a website, you need to give the date that you visited the website and the website address. If you use an article on the website, write down the author, the title of the article, and the copyright. This makes it easier to go back to where you found the information. It also gives credit to the author for his work.

Marco took notes from a book he read about engineers. This is how he wrote his note card.

Source {

> *What's It Like to Be an Engineer?*      Page 10
>
> by Zachary Thomas    (Career Publications, 2010)
>
> There are many different types of engineers: civil, } Fact
>
> electrical, biomedical, mechanical.

You can **summarize** what you have read by listing the main points and details. Or, you might decide to paraphrase what you have read. When you **paraphrase,** you put the information into your own words.

Marco took notes on what he read about his topic. He put much of the information in his own words. However, he put the information that he was quoting directly into quotation marks. Marco also noted where he found his information. This will help him later when he credits his sources. Marco's sources included an interview with his dad, the website of an engineering society, and a book about engineering.

> "I love my job because I use different skills each day. I need to know math, computer programs, and how to work as a team."

Why did Marco put information that he quoted from his source in quotation marks?

_____

_____

 Notes should be accurate. Paraphrasing or summarizing the information in your own words is fine. However, it is important to give people credit for their work or what they have said. Here is a sample answer:

The quotation marks indicate that this information is someone else's work and it is in his or her words. Later, this will help Marco when he needs to use quotations in his paper. It will also help him avoid taking credit for someone else's work.

What information should Marco include on his note card when he credits his interview with his father?

_____

_____

_____

_____

 When a printed source such as a book is being credited, you would give information about the author, the title of the book, the publisher, and the publication date. All sources should include similar information. Here is a sample answer:

*Marco should note that it was a personal interview. He should tell who he interviewed and the date he interviewed the person.*

Which of these is the *best* way for Marco to cite his interview with his father?

A   Dad, personal interview

B   Dad, yesterday, personal interview

C   March 14, 2011, interview

D   Raymond Ramos, personal interview, March 14, 2011

 Your note card should have as much information as possible. This makes it easy to go back to the source. Choice D is the correct answer. Choices A, B, and C do not give all the important information.

# Test Yourself

Mya is writing a research paper about the Mason-Dixon line. This line divides the northern states from the southern states. This boundry was important during the Civil War. Mya learned that the line was created well before the Civil War. The line was named for the men who created it. Charles Mason and Jeremiah Dixon mapped out the line in 1763. It solved the argument Maryland and Pennsylvania were having over the border between the two colonies. Mya learned that the Mason-Dixon line will celebrate an anniversary in 2013. She also learned that an organization is working to preserve the mile markers along the line.

1  Which of the following is a secondary source that Mya might use for her research?

   A   diary

   B   letter

   C   document

   D   magazine

2  Where should Mya look to find out more about the mile markers?

   A   a book about the Civil War

   B   the website of the Maryland archives

   C   the letter announcing the anniversary celebration

   D   the website of the organization preserving the mile markers

3  Mya wants to find out when the anniversary celebration will take place. Which of the following would be a good resource to use?

   A   www.m-dlinecelebration.org

   B   www.dixonuniversity.edu

   C   www.maryland.com

   D   www.mason.com

**4** Mya read an article about the Mason-Dixon line, then took notes on what she read. Read the article on page 142 and then use these cards to take notes on what you have read.

# Mason-Dixon Line

by John Sampson

In colonial days, the future American states did not always have exact borders. Sometimes natural features like rivers or mountains divided colonies. In other cases, the boundaries were not clear. As a result, kings sometimes gave the same land to two different colonies. This caused problems. That's what happened between the Penn family of Pennsylvania and the Calvert family of Maryland.

In the early 1700s, the dividing line between Maryland and Pennsylvania was not clear. No one knew exactly where one colony ended and the other began. Both colonies argued over the border. To fix this problem, they went to court in 1750. A judge ruled that the border between the two colonies ran along the line of 37 degrees, 43 minutes north latitude. But exactly where did this line lie?

Surveyors tried to map the line. However, the border between the two colonies was hard to survey. The Appalachian Mountains in the western part of the colonies made it harder to determine the boundary. In 1763, two English experts were called in. Charles Mason was an astronomer. Jeremiah Dixon was a surveyor.

Their job was not easy because they had to travel through the wilderness. There were no roads. The men mapped out the line using the stars to measure their location. This meant they had to bring along a six-foot-long telescope. They also brought large stones with them to mark the line they mapped out.

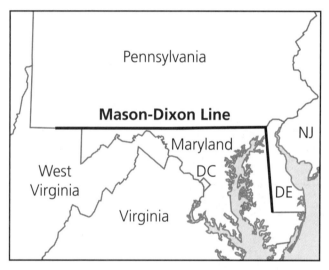

They placed these stones every mile to mark the boundary. The stones had a letter *P* for Pennsylvania on the north face and a letter *M* for Maryland on the south face. Every five miles they placed larger crownstones. These stones had the Penn coat of arms on one side and the Calvert coat of arms on the other. The project took the two men five years to complete. Together, they mapped out a line 244 miles long. This border ran 15 miles south of Philadelphia to the west. The Mason-Dixon line marks the border between Maryland and Pennsylvania to this day. If you travel along this border, you can still see the stones that Mason and Dixon placed to mark this boundary.

# Outlining the Research Paper

W.5.2, 4, 6–9

Selecting a topic and doing research about the topic are the first two steps in writing your research paper. The third step is to organize the information that you have found. You want to decide on a main point for your paper. Then you want to use the information you researched to support the main point of your paper. If you find that you need more information, you can continue researching your topic.

## Step 3: Determine the Thesis Statement

The **thesis statement** sums up the main point of your paper. It tells the purpose of your paper. It is like the main idea or topic sentence that you learned about in Lesson 3. The thesis statement should be specific. It should have one main point. Your research paper will support the thesis statement with examples and evidence. The thesis statement should appear at the end of your opening paragraph.

Keep in mind that your thesis statement may change. Sometimes when you do research you find that your argument is no longer valid. Or, maybe you want to write about a different aspect than what you intended. You can always revise your thesis statement. However, the thesis statement must be related to what you discuss in your paper. It sets out the direction in which you are going.

Depending on the type of research paper, the thesis statement might set out your position on an issue. Or, it might offer a hypothesis that your paper will prove.

# Guided Practice

Marco is writing a research paper on a career that interests him. He has decided to write about engineering. His dad is an engineer. Marco has interviewed him for the paper. He has also used other materials to find out more about what an engineer does and engineering as a career.

Which of these statements would be a good thesis statement for Marco's research paper?

A   My dad is an engineer.

B   I want to be an engineer.

C   Here is my report on a career.

D   Engineering is a good choice for a career.

A good thesis statement gives the main point. The thesis statement should not be a fact. This is too limiting. The thesis statement needs to suggest that the paper will support the statement. Choices A, B, and C are facts. Choice D is a good thesis statement. The paper can now explain why engineering is a good choice for a career. It would include information about what an engineer does. It would also explain why it is a good choice. Maybe it pays well or there may be lots of jobs available.

## Step 4: Outline the Paper

Once you have determined the main point or purpose of your paper, then you are ready to being organizing your paper. Research papers are typically longer than the other types of writing that you do. An outline will help you to organize both your research and what you want to say. You can begin by outlining the main points that support your thesis, and then organize your research to match these points. Or, you could begin by sorting through your research and then determining your outline. You may find in creating your outline that you need more information to support a main idea. There may be more information than you can use. The outline helps you to organize your thinking. It is a road map for writing your paper.

For your outline, use roman numerals or ABC for your main ideas. Then under the main ideas list the points or details that support the main idea. Here is an example on an outline:

I. Introduction
    A. Opening statement
    B. Thesis statement

II. Body
    A. Main Idea
        1. Detail
        2. Detail
    B. Main Idea
        1. Detail
        2. Detail
    C. Main Idea
        1. Detail
        2. Detail

III. Conclusion
    A. Clincher
    B. Restatement of thesis
    C. Concluding statement

## Guided Practice

**Read the passage. Then create an outline.**

After Marco finishes researching his topic, his next step is to create an outline. Fill in the outline based on the information from Marco's research.

Marco has learned many things about an engineering career. He has learned what education and training an engineer needs. Marco also knows how much money an engineer can make and how many engineers will be needed in the future. His dad explained what an engineer does in a typical day. Marco has also learned about the different types of engineers. Now, he is ready to outline the main points he will cover in his paper.

What headings could Marco use for the main part of his paper? Fill in the outline.

I. Introduction
    A. Opening statement
    B. Thesis statement: *Engineering is a good choice for a career.*

II. Body
    A. _____
        1. Detail
        2. Detail
    B. _____
        1. Detail
        2. Detail
    C. _____
        1. Detail
        2. Detail

 **Think about the main points Mario wants to cover in his paper. If you were going to be an engineer, what would you like to know about this career? Here is a sample answer:**

I. Introduction
    A. Opening statement
    B. Thesis statement: *Engineering is a good choice for a career.*
II. Body
    A. Education and Training
        1. College degree in engineering
        2. Internship
    B. Duties and Responsibilities
        1. Work as a team
        2. Oversee projects
    C. Earnings and Future Openings
        1. $55,000 –$100,000
        2. Strong need for engineers

When you are satisfied that you have all the information you need and that your outline shows how you will support or prove your thesis statement, then you are ready to write your paper.

# Test Yourself

Mya is writing a research paper about the Mason-Dixon line. This line divides the northern states from the southern states. This line was important during the Civil War. Mya learned that the line was created well before the Civil War. The line was named for the men who created it. Charles Mason and Jeremiah Dixon created the line in 1763. It solved the argument Maryland and Pennsylvania were having over the border between the two colonies. Mya learned that the Mason-Dixon line will celebrate an anniversary in 2013. She also learned that an organization is working to preserve the mile markers along the line.

**1** Write an outline that Mya might use for her paper. Use the information above to help determine the main points in the body of her report.

I. Introduction

II. Body

A. _____

    1._____

    2._____

B. _____

    1._____

    2._____

C. _____

    1._____

    2._____

**2** Where should the thesis statement appear in the research paper?

    **A**  in the conclusion

    **B**  in every paragraph

    **C**  in the second paragraph

    **D**  at the end of the opening paragraph

**3** Write a thesis statement for Mya's research paper.

_____

_____

_____

_____

# 12

# Writing the Research Paper

W.5.2, 4, 6–9

First, you decided on your topic, then you researched the topic. Next, you developed a thesis statement that explained the purpose of your paper. The outline helped you decide on the structure for your paper. Now, you are ready to begin writing the draft of your paper.

## Step 5: Write the Paper

Writing the research paper uses the same writing process as you learned in Lesson 1. You want to plan your paper, write your draft, then revise and edit the paper, and publish it. You might decide to include visual materials in you paper. Think about what would help the reader. If you are writing about a particular place, a map might be helpful. If you are giving the reader facts and figures, a graph or chart might make this information easier to understand. A science research paper might include a diagram to help the reader.

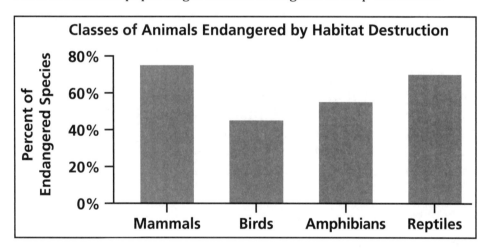

Massachusetts Bay Colony

# Guided Practice

**Read the passage. Then answer the questions.**

Marco wants to include some visual aids in his research paper. There are different types of engineers and he wants to show examples of the projects they work on. He knows a civil engineer works on roads, houses, and other buildings. An electronics engineer helps create computers and other electronics. Chemical engineers develop new products and ways to make these products safely. An aerospace engineer creates things used in space. An electrical engineer works with electricity.

Which of these could Marco use to show what a civil engineer works on?

**A** a drawing of a power grid

**B** a photograph of a bridge

**C** a diagram of a spaceship

**D** a chart listing new food products

Choice B is the correct answer. A civil engineer helps build bridges. Choices A, C, and D are incorrect. An electrical engineer would work with a drawing of a power grid. Aerospace engineers would use a diagram of a spaceship. A chemical engineer may have been involved in creating new food products.

What other visual aids could Marco include in his paper?

_____

_____

_____

_____

Any visuals used in a research paper should give the reader more information. The visual aids should support the information in the research paper. Graphs, charts, lists, photographs, and diagrams are types of visuals often used in a paper. Here is a sample answer:

Marco could create a table that lists the different types of engineers.

**Types of Engineers**

Aerospace Engineers

Agricultural Engineers

Chemical Engineers

Civil Engineers

Mining Engineers

Nuclear Engineers

Petroleum Engineers

# Step 6: Create a Source List

An important part of the research paper is sharing what you've discovered and giving credit where it is due. If you have kept track of your sources on your note cards, then it will be easier to create your source list.

The source list is an important part of the research paper. Readers can use the source list to see where you found your information. They can use it to find out more information about the facts you presented in your paper. This may help them find sources for their own work.

The source list is usually presented the same way. Sources are listed in alphabetical order by last name. A source listing should include who wrote it, what they wrote, when they wrote, and who published it, and where the publisher is located. Here is an example:

Author last name, author first name. Title of work. City of publication: Publication company, publication date.

Most of this information is on the title page or the copyright page. The title page lists the name of the book, the author, and the publisher. The copyright is the date that the book was published. This is on the copyright page, which is the back of the title page.

If you are citing information from the Internet, then you want the author, the title of the article or the website, then give the publication date, the date that you found the information, and the website address. Here is an example:

Author last name, author first name. Title of work (or website). Copyright date. Retrieved date retrieved, <website address>.

Marco used these sources to create his paper. He also used a personal interview with his father. This is the source list he created. He used the source number on some of his note cards.

## Source List

Source 1 Book
Thomas, Zachary. *What's It Like to Be an Engineer?* New York: Career Publications, 2010.

Source 2 Website
Craig, David. "What Engineers Do." www.societyofengineers.org. 2010. Retrieved 10 March 2011, <www.societyofengineers.org>.

Source 3 Encyclopedia
"Engineer." *Encyclopedia Britannica,* vol. 3, 2011.

Source 4 Magazine
Peters, Kelly. "Top 10 Engineers." *Engineering Today* magazine. Jan/Feb 2010.

Source 5 Personal Interview
Ramos, Raymond. Personal interview. March 14, 2011. Personal residence.

# Guided Practice

Marco used a number of sources for his research paper. He used a couple books about engineers. Marco also interviewed his father about his job. An encyclopedia was another source he found helpful. He read the entry for engineer in volume 3 of the *Encyclopedia Britannica* to get a general idea about this career. There are many editions of this encyclopedia but Marco used the current edition, 2011. The *Republican-Herald* newspaper also had an article on May 6, 2011 titled "What Do Engineers Do?" that Marco used. The author was Peter Fossil.

Which of the following is the correct way to list an encyclopedia source?

A  "Engineer." *Encyclopedia Britannica,* vol. 3, 2011.

B  *Encyclopedia Britannica,* vol. 3, 2011.

C  2011. Vol 3. "Engineer." *Encyclopedia Britannica*

D  *Encyclopedia Britannica, Engineer, 2011, volume 3*

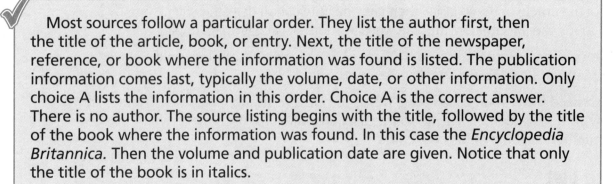

Most sources follow a particular order. They list the author first, then the title of the article, book, or entry. Next, the title of the newspaper, reference, or book where the information was found is listed. The publication information comes last, typically the volume, date, or other information. Only choice A lists the information in this order. Choice A is the correct answer. There is no author. The source listing begins with the title, followed by the title of the book where the information was found. In this case the *Encyclopedia Britannica.* Then the volume and publication date are given. Notice that only the title of the book is in italics.

Which is the correct way to list a newspaper source?

A   Fossil, Peter. "What Do Engineers Do?" *Republican-Herald,* 6 May 2011.

B   *Republican-Herald,* 6 May 2011, "What Do Engineers Do?" by Peter Fossil.

C   "What Do Engineers Do? 6 May 2011 Republican-Herald by Peter Fossil.

D   6 May 2011, *Republican-Herald,* Peter Fossil, "What Do Engineers Do?"

The source listing for a newspaper article is similar to that of a book. The author is listed first, then the title of the article, then the location where the article appeared, and the publication date. Choice A is the correct answer. It lists the information in this order.

## Publishing the Research Paper

Once you have written your draft, the next steps are the same as those you learned in Lesson 1. You may need to revise your paper to add information, quotations, or other information. Or, you may need to revise what you've written to make it clearer. When you are satisfied with the organization and content, then you can edit it.

You might also decide that you want to include visual materials. Put yourself in the reader's shoes. If you knew nothing about the subject, what visual material can make a point clearer or add additional support. Perhaps, a map would help a reader understand the location being discussed. A diagram might reinforce the text.

Your paper can be published in many ways. It might include a cover page and be turned into your teacher. Or, you might use the information to create a PowerPoint, a poster, or a brochure. You can also adapt your research paper to present as a speech. Another way to publish your paper is by creating a display.

# Test Yourself

1   Mya needs to include visual aids in her report about the Mason-Dixon line. Which of the following would be a good choice to explain where the line is located?

   A   map of the United States

   B   portrait of William Penn

   C   photograph of the Calvert coat of arms

   D   map showing the Mason-Dixon line

2   What type of visual aid might Mya use to show what a crownstone or mile marker looks like?

   _____

   _____

   _____

   _____

   _____

3   Name two other visual aids that Mya might include in her paper about the Mason-Dixon line.

   1. _____

   2. _____

4   Which of these is the correct way to credit a book source?

   A   Adams, Joshua. *Engineers.* New York: Harper, 2010.

   B   Joshua Adams. *Engineers.* New York: 2010, Harper.

   C   *Engineers.* Joshua Adams. New York: 2010, Harper.

   D   *Engineers.* Adams, Joshua. New York: 2010, Harper.

# Language Conventions

UNIT
4

Good writing starts with good sentence structure and word choices. This unit reviews the rules and conventions that help you write clear sentences.

- **In Lesson 13,** you will review the grammar rules you have learned. These rules help you to write clear sentences. You will make sure that subjects and verbs agree. You will check that pronoun forms are correct.

- **Lesson 14** covers standard English conventions. You will review punctuation and capitalization rules. This will help you recognize that titles are capitalized or in quotes and that punctuation marks are used correctly.

# Language Conventions

**W.5.5, L.5.3**

Good writing starts with good sentences. Choosing the right word is important in writing. Correctly using punctuation and possessives is also important to creating good sentences.

## Comma

A **comma** is used to separate the speaker and verbs such as *said, asked, answered,* and *exclaimed.* If the speaker comes before the quotation, a comma follows the verb.

> Kmiko said, "I want to be an engineer."

If the speaker comes after the quotation, and there is no question mark or exclamation point, a comma is used before the quotation mark.

> "This backpack is very heavy," said Steven.

A comma is used to separate the name of a person being spoken to from the rest of the sentence.

> Jessie, are you going home now?
> I'll be leaving in a minute, Ben.

A comma is used after words that introduce a sentence or connect it back to the sentence that came before. Sometimes these are single words like *yes, no, well, indeed, however,* and *therefore.*

> Yes, I'd like to see the basketball game.
> However, I may have to clean my room on Saturday.

A comma is also used to separate another question that is part of a sentence.

> That's you calling me, isn't it, Jared?

A comma is used to separate an introductory element from the rest of a sentence.

> Today, I will be leaving for vacation.

A comma is used to separate items in a series.

> The United States flag is red, white, and blue.

# Guided Practice

**Read the sentences. Then rewrite the sentence adding the commas as needed.**

Pasta rice and potatoes are starches.

_____

 A comma should be used between the items in a series. Here is the correct answer:

> Pasta, rice, and potatoes are starches.

Well look who's here!

_____

 A comma should be used to set off introductory words or phrases that appear at the beginning of a sentence. Here is the correct answer:

> Well, look who's here!

Who are you calling your father?

_____

 This sentence asks two questions. A comma is used to set off a question that appears in a sentence. Here is the correct answer:

> Who are you calling, your father?

## Quotation Marks

Quotation marks are used before and after the titles of short works
such as stories, poems, magazine articles, chapters in a book, songs, or TV
shows.

STORY: "The Necklace"
POEM: "Chicago"
CHAPTER: "After the Revolution"
SONG: "America the Beautiful"
TV SHOW: "American Idol"

The titles of longer works such as books, magazines, movies, and plays are underlined or put in italics.

BOOK: *Ramona the Pest*
MAGAZINE: *Smithsonian*
NEWSPAPER: *The New York Times*
MOVIE: *Charlie and the Chocolate Factory*
PLAY: *Grease*

# Guided Practice

**Use the correct punctuation in the titles in each sentence below.**

Movies did not have sound until The Jazz Singer was made in 1927.

 You can tell from the sentence that the movie title is being used. Here is the correct answer:

Movies did not have sound until *The Jazz Singer* was made in 1927.

Are you going to see the high school production of Romeo and Juliet?

 The high school production most likely refers to a play rather than a movie. Note where the question mark belongs in this sentence. Here is the correct answer:

Are you going to see the high school production of "Romeo and Juliet"?

The Celebrated Jumping Frog of Calaveras County was one of Mark Twain's earliest stories.

 Think about how you treat the title of a story. What punctuation do you use? Here is the correct answer:

"The Celebrated Jumping Frog of Calaveras County" was one of Mark Twain's earliest stories.

**UNIT 4** ▨▨▨▨▨▨▨▨▨▨▨▨▨▨▨▨▨▨▨▨▨▨▨▨▨▨▨▨▨▨▨▨▨▨▨
Language Conventions

# Possessives

A possessive noun shows ownership. A noun can be made to show ownership by changing its form.

> A picture of my **family** is on the desk. (noun)
> My **family's** picture is on the desk. (possessive noun)

To make a singular noun possessive add an apostrophe and an -*s* as you did to family. A singular noun that ends in *s* still has an apostrophe and an -*s* added.

> **Hilda's** gloves are on the table.
> Mrs. **Kass's** tulips are blooming.

To make a plural noun that ends in *s* possessive add an apostrophe only.

> The **students'** reports were on display.
> The **Smiths'** house was being painted.

To make a plural noun that does not end in *s* a possessive noun, add an apostrophe and an -*s*.

> The **children's** notebooks were collected for review.
> The **mice's** footsteps could be heard.

Sometimes it is hard to tell if a word is a possessive noun or a plural noun just by hearing the word spoken. For example, *teachers, teacher's,* and *teachers'* all sound the same. However, by looking at the spelling of the word and the way the word is used in a sentence, you can determine what it is.

> The **teachers** are meeting today. (plural noun)
> The **teacher's** meeting is today. (singular possessive noun)
> The **teachers'** meeting is today. (plural possessive noun)

# Guided Practice

The _____ croaking was very loud. (frog)

The _____ wings are used for flight. (birds)

The _____ hat blew off in the gust of wind. (woman)

The _____ performance pleased the crowd. (band)

The _____ house is newly painted. (Joneses)

**Note whether the noun is singular or plural. Here are the correct answers:**

The _____frog's_____ croaking was very loud. (frog)

The _____birds'_____ wings are used for flight. (birds)

The _____woman's_____ hat blew off in the gust of wind. (woman)

The _____band's_____ performance pleased the crowd. (band)

The _____Joneses'_____ house is newly painted. (Joneses)

## Possessive Pronouns

Possessive pronouns are pronouns that show possession or ownership of something. Just as subject pronouns replace nouns as subjects, so possessive pronouns replace nouns that show possession.

> Miranda washed **Miranda's** dishes. (possessive noun)
> Miranda washed **her** dishes. (possessive pronoun)

Singular possessive nouns are *my, mine, your, yours, his, her, hers, its.*
Plural possessive nouns are *our, ours, your, yours, their, theirs.*

Some of these possessive pronouns are always used with nouns. These include *my, your, his, her, its, our, their.*

Other possessive pronouns always stand alone, which means nouns do not follow them. These include *mine, yours, his, hers, its, ours, theirs.*

> I think that notebook is **mine.**
> This is my blue jacket. **Hers** is on the chair.

# Guided Practice

In each sentence, underline the possessive noun. On the line at the right, replace the possessive noun with the correct possessive pronoun.

The winning poster is Mike's and Todd's. _____

The library's books are on the shelves. _____

He used blue paint for the children's room. _____

✓ **Did you answer correctly? Here are the correct answers:**

The winning poster is Mike's and Todd's. ____theirs____

The library's books are on the shelves. ____Its____

He used blue paint for the children's room. ____their____

# Test Yourself

Early forms of transportation included wagon trains, Thousands of
people traveled across the plains and over the mountains in canvas
covered wagons. most of the passengers were heading west because
of the California Gold Rush. Everyone wanted to get rich quickly?
Many did not make it and the trails became littered with broken
wagons dead animals and human skeletons. Do you think you would
have enjoyed traveling by wagon trains.

**Replace each underlined group of words with a possessive noun.**

1. the chalk belonging <u>to the teacher</u> _____

2. the whistles belonging <u>to the coaches</u> _____

3. the jacket worn <u>by Mr. Gross</u> _____

4. the dew drops <u>on the leaves</u> _____

5. the books belonging <u>to the children</u> _____

Beth knows that ants is fascinating to watch, so he decided to build an ant farm. Beths' friends wants to help. They ask she what materials to use. Beth tells they to gather the things on hers list. Her will supervise the building of the ant farm with the friend's materials. Beth and her friends researches ants to learn more about it. The friends or Beth plan to make a poster about ants. The girl's research has taught them that ants live in colonies, and different kinds of ants has different jobs. The queen lays eggs. She is larger than the other ants. Worker ants take care of hers. Soldier ants protect the colony. Beth and her friends also learn that some ants bite. Beth tells her friends, "Me and you will have to be careful! Us don't want to get bitten!"

Although Andrews mother (tell, tells) he is it not a good idea to bring his computer to school, him (does, do) so anyway. At school he (try, tries) to be very careful, but he accidentally (bumps, bump) into the table and (knock, knocks) the computer onto the floor. Her friends (gasp, gasps) when it falls. The teacher (hope, hopes) that the fall hasn't broken its. Although it (seems, seem) fine, the screen (remain, remains) dark. Andrew is very worried. Then one of his friends (call, calls) to him from across the room. "Look!" he (exclaims, exclaim). "The screens' cord is unplugged." Andrew (plug, plugs) in the cord, and the computer (come, comes) to life. He tells him friends, "Now me and you can do our work."

# Grammar

W.5.5, L.5.2

Sentences are the building blocks of writing. A sentence is a group of words that expresses a complete thought.

Every sentence has two parts: a subject and a complete predicate. The subject tells the person, place, thing, or idea that a sentence is about. It also tells who or what is doing the action in a sentence. The predicate tells something about the subject. It identifies what the subject does, is, has, or feels.

Our teacher <u>wants us to turn in a permission form</u>.

The subject in the sentence above is *Our teacher*.
The predicate is <u>wants us to turn in a permission form</u>.

**A complete subject** can be one word or several words. The key word in the complete subject is the simple subject. It identifies what the subject is about. The simple subject is often a **noun,** although sometimes the subject is a pronoun.

**Subject Pronouns**
**Singular  Plural**

| I | we | <u>She</u> filled out the permission form. |
| you | you | <u>It</u> was easy to fill out |
| he, she, it | they | <u>We</u> will turn it in tomorrow. |

**A complete predicate,** like a complete subject, can be one word or several words. The key word in the complete predicate is the simple predicate, or **verb.** The verb may be a single word, or it may have a helping verb.

Birds sing.        The birds <u>are singing</u>.

# Guided Practice

Which of the following is the subject of the sentence?

*They left early today for the field trip.*

A   They

B   today

C   field trip

D   early

> The subject in a sentence is a noun or pronoun. The correct answer is choice A. Choices B, C, and D are part of the predicate.

Which of the following is the predicate?

*The football team has an away game tomorrow.*

A   The football team has

B   has an away game

C   team has an away game tomorrow

D   has an away game tomorrow

> The verb in this sentence is *has.* You can tell that the complete predicate is choice D. This explains what action the subject is taking.

Verbs such as *sing* are called **action verbs.** Action verbs are sometimes followed by an object. An object, like a subject, is often a noun and can be one word or several words. The object receives the action of the verb. Look at the object nouns underlined in these sentences.

I play the piano.

We sing "The Star-Spangled Banner" during assembly.

An object can also be a pronoun. Look at the object pronouns underlined in these sentences.

**Object Pronouns**

| Singular | Plural | |
|---|---|---|
| me | us | We sing <u>it</u> every day. |
| you | you | Jared heard <u>them</u> outside. |
| him, her, it | them | |

Verbs such as *is*, *were*, and *seem* are called **linking verbs.** The verb "links" the subject and the noun after the verb. Here each linking verb is in bold type, and the noun it connects to the subject is underlined.

Those books **are** <u>novels</u>.　　　Lara **is** a <u>heroine</u> in that novel.

# Guided Practice

**Read the sentences. Then answer the questions.**

Which of the following sentences has an action verb?

**A**　Randy ran quickly to first base.

**B**　The star of the play is Amanda.

**C**　This book is a quick read.

**D**　Here is the money for the shirt.

> Choice A is the correct answer. The verb *ran* describes an action that the subject is performing. Choices B, C, and D are linking verbs.

Which of the following sentences has a linking verb?

**A**　She is a good dancer.

**B**　Frank won the election.

**C**　Kanesha loves playing soccer.

**D**　Kathleen bought her ticket to the dance.

> A linking verb joins the subject and the noun that follows the verb. Choice A is the correct answer. The verb *is* joins the subject (She) with the noun after the verb (dancer). The other choices have action verbs.

# Subject and Verb Agreement

For a sentence to be correct, the subject and the verb must agree in number. That means that if the subject is singular, the verb must be singular. If the subject is plural, the verb must be plural. Remember, singular means one; plural means more than one. In the following examples, the subject is underlined once, and each verb is underlined twice.

> The horse pulls the wagon. (singular)
> Two horses pull the plow. (plural)

Generally, singular verbs in the present tense end in *s* or *es*.
> The student finishes her homework. (singular)

Plural verbs in the present tense do not end in *s* or *es*.
> The students finish their homework. (plural)

However, if the singular subject is *I* or *you,* this rule does not apply. The verb does not end in *s* or *es*.
> I finish my homework. (singular)

A compound subject is two or more simple subjects joined by *and* or *or.* A compound subject and its verb must also agree in number. When the subjects are joined by *and,* the verb is plural. This is true whether the subjects themselves are singular or plural.

> Los Angeles *and* San Francisco are in California. (two singular subjects)
> Apples *and* oranges are popular fruits. (two plural subjects)

A compound predicate is two or more simple predicates joined by *and* or *or.* The verbs in a compound predicate must agree in number with the subject.

> The airplane makes a loud roar *and* rises off the ground. (singular)
> The freshly baked cookies smell great *and* taste good. (plural)

# Guided Practice

**Read each sentence. Then circle the correct verb or subject in parentheses.**

Many children (like, likes) to play video games.

A young child easily (learn, learns) to use a mouse.

The (river, rivers) flows right near my house.

The (neighbor, neighbors) sometimes join us for a swim.

 A singular subject takes a singular verb. Did you answer correctly? Here are the correct answers:

Many children (**like,** likes) to play video games.

A young child easily (learn, **learns**) to use a mouse.

The (**river,** rivers) flows right near my house.

The (neighbor, **neighbors**) sometimes join us for a swim.

## Fragments

A sentence needs both a subject and a predicate to express a complete thought. If one or both of these is missing, the sentence is incomplete. An incomplete sentence is called a sentence fragment.

Although a fragment may begin with a capital letter and end with a punctuation mark, it is not a sentence. A fragment may lack a subject, a predicate, or both.

# Guided Practice

**Read the sentence. Then select the answer that best describes the sentence.**

The dog in the house.

   **A**   This is missing a predicate.

   **B**   This is missing a subject.

   **C**   This is missing both a subject and a predicate.

   **D**   This is a complete sentence.

 A complete sentence must have both a subject that is doing the action and a predicate that tells about the subject.  The dog in the house is the subject. However, there is no predicate. Choice A is the correct answer.

**168**

**UNIT 4** :::::::::::::::::::::::::::::::::::::::::::::::::::::::::::
Language Conventions

© The Continental Press, Inc.   DUPLICATING THIS MATERIAL IS ILLEGAL.

_____ Aardvarks are similar to anteaters.

_____ In many ways.

_____ Aardvarks live in Africa.

_____ Feed mostly on ants and termites.

A sentence must have both a subject and a verb. Did you identify the fragments? Here are the correct answers:

_____S_____ Aardvarks are similar to anteaters.

_____F_____ In many ways.

_____S_____ Aardvarks live in Africa.

_____F_____ Feed mostly on ants and termites.

## Run-on Sentence

A run-on sentence is two or more sentences that run together with commas or without any punctuation. This creates confusion because a reader does not know where one thought ends and the next thought begins.

> We will have to hurry now, we will be late. (comma)
> We will have to hurry now we will be late. (no punctuation)

There are two ways to correct a run-on sentence. One way is to write a complete thought as a separate sentence.

> We will have to hurry now. We will be late.

Another way is to use a conjunction to combine each complete thought to create a compound sentence. A compound sentence is made up of two simple sentences that are joined by a comma and a conjunction such as _and, or, but,_ or _so._

> We will have to hurry now, or we will be late.

# Guided Practice

Kirsten likes to sing she also loves to dance.

The Carey family cooked the turkey we brought the pies.

 First, identify the subject. Then identify the verb. This will help you correct a run-on sentence:

Kirsten likes to sing. She also loves to dance.
Kirsten likes to sing and dance.

The Carey family cooked the turkey. We brought the pies.
The Carey family cooked the turkey, and we brought the pies.

## Shifts in Verb Tense

Verb tense has to do with time. They help the reader know when something took place. Verb tense can reveal the time when something occurred or the sequence in which events happened. They also reveal the state or condition when used with linking verbs. Avoid changing verb tenses when you write.

There are three main divisions: the past, the present, and the future. The progressive verb tense shows an action in progress.

I was walking to school when I saw Tim. (past progressive)
I am walking to school today. (present progressive)
I will be walking to school in the next half hour. (future progressive)

The perfect verb tense shows actions that occurred in the past.

I had walked to school last week with Tim. (past perfect)
I have walked to school with Tim before. (present perfect)
I will have walked to school for three months. (future perfect)

The present perfect is a past action that occurred at some point in the past. Or, it is an action that began in that past and continues in the present. This is formed with either the verb *has* or *have* and the past participle that ends in *-ed*.

I have walked past his house twice.

The past perfect is an action that was completed before another past action. This is formed by using the verb *had* and the past participle of the verb.

> I had walked by his house last night before he called.

The future perfect tense is an action completed before a set future time. An action needs to occur before another action. This tense is formed with the verb *will have* and the past participle of the verb.

> I will have walked around the block twice before supper.

# Guided Practice

**Read the sentences. Then write the correct verb on the line.**

1. The soccer player ran, received the pass from his teammate, and then scores. _____

2. Kevin opens the cupboard door, grabbed the cereal, and then poured the cereal in a bowl. _____

3. Kelly watches her brother as he played with his trucks. _____

4. The teacher said, "Pass the papers back and then turned over the paper until I say begin." _____

> Think about when the action happened. Then make sure the tense matches the time when the action occurred. Here are the correct answers:

1. *scored* not scores
2. *opened* not opens
3. *watched* not watches or *plays* not played
4. *turn* not turned

# Conjunctions

Conjunctions are connecting words. They can join two subjects. Or, they can join two complete sentences to create a compound subject. Some conjunctions include *and, or, but,* or *so.* Correlative conjunctions like *either/or, neither/nor, not only/but also* are used in pairs. The elements that follow them should be parallel.

> Karen is **not only** kind **but also** helpful.

> Do you want to get **either** Chinese food **or** Italian food for dinner?

# Guided Practice

**Read the sentences. Then write the correct punctuation and conjunction (and, or, but, so).**

Some people say 45 degrees Fahrenheit is cold _____ others say 0 degrees Fahrenheit is cold.

Snow can make roads slippery _____ drivers need to slow down in a snowstorm.

Winter in northern states can be six months long _____ it can be very windy or cold.

 A comma usually comes before a conjunction. Did you use the correct conjunctions? Here are the correct answers:

Some people say 45 degrees Fahrenheit is cold, _but_ others say 0 degrees Fahrenheit is cold.

Snow can make roads slippery, _so_ drivers need to slow down in a snowstorm.

Winter in northern states can be six months long, _and_ it can be very windy or cold.

## Prepositional Phrases

A prepositional phrase is a group of words that begins with a preposition (*of, in, on, to, into, for, at, from, with*, and *by*) and ends with its object, which is a noun. A prepositional phrase may also include words that describe its object.

Compare the following prepositional phrases. In each phrase the preposition is in bold type and its object is underlined. Notice the words used to describe the object in the second example for each phrase.

**in** the <u>park</u>          **in** the city's new <u>park</u>
**up** a <u>tree</u>          **up** a large oak <u>tree</u>

Sometimes you can combine two sentences by changing one of them into a prepositional phrase. Then you can add the phrase to the sentence that comes either before or after it.

The troop camped out overnight. They camped **in the park.**
The troop camped out overnight **in the park.**

**UNIT 4** ▦▦▦▦▦▦▦▦▦▦▦▦▦▦▦▦▦▦▦▦▦▦▦▦▦▦
Language Conventions

# Guided Practice

I spotted the frog at the other end of the pond.

My mother is starting a new job in the fall.

Her family lives in a log cabin in the woods.

> Prepositional phrases begin with prepositions like *in, on, up, of,* and *at.*
> **Here are the correct answers:**

at the other end of the pond

in the fall

in a log cabin

in the woods

## Precise Words

The words you choose and the sentences you write can make your meaning clear—or they can give the wrong message. Use precise verbs and nouns when you write.

Look at the following sentence. What other words could be used in place of the verb *jumped?*

Suddenly, the horse jumped over the wall.

The word *suddenly* gives you a hint. It tells you that the horse moved quickly and unexpectedly. The horse might have *bolted, leaped, bounded,* or even *crashed.* Each verb provides a different picture of how the horse jumped.

# Guided Practice

We <u>walked</u> along the beach.

The fifth grade students <u>showed</u> their drawings.

The airplane <u>moved</u> down the runway.

> Adjectives describe nouns or pronouns. The more specific your adjectives are, the better your writing will be. Here are some sample answers:

We <u>strolled</u> along the beach.

The fifth grade students <u>exhibited</u> their drawings.

The airplane <u>taxied</u> down the runway.

# Test Yourself

1 The founding fathers of the United States adopted a system of government similar to that of the ancient Greeks.

2 They wanted a democracy.

3 Our federal government has three branches.

4 Each branch can check the decisions of the other branches.

5 This arrangement is called the system of checks and balances.

**Use specific adjectives to complete each sentence.**

6 The _____ horses grazed on the prairie beneath the _____ sky.

7 Visiting the _____ building was a(n) _____ adventure for the whole family.

8 The _____ drizzle kept the _____ children in the house all day.

**Read each sentence. Then circle the correct verb in parentheses.**

9 A plumber (fix, fixes) a water leak.

10 Word games and video games (is, are) fun to play on the computer.

11 Libraries (have, has) computers available for Internet searches.

**Read the sentence. Then circle the correct subject in parentheses.**

**12** The (rock, rocks) are sometimes slippery.

**13** My (leg, legs) has a bruise from the last time I fell in the water.

**14** My (friend, friends) were worried that I would drown.

**Edit the paragraph.**

Trains are an important part. Of the transportation network. Across American and around the world. They move both people and things from place to place. Carry freight to major centers. The freight is then moved to trucks. Take it to specific destinations.

Some people prefer traveling in trains. Train travel is slower than flying most riders don't mind because trains are more comfortable train travel is cheaper.

# Test-Taking Tips

You are about to take a writing test. Before you begin, review these tips for taking a test.

## Prepare ahead of time.
- Bring more than one pen or pencil. Be sure they work!
- Get plenty of sleep the night before.
- Eat a good breakfast on the morning of the test.

## Budget your time.
- Spend most of your time on planning and drafting.
- Make a schedule based on the time available. For example, if you have one hour, figure 5 minutes for reading the question, 10 minutes for planning, 30 minutes for drafting, and 15 minutes for revising and proofreading.
- Check the clock during the test. Are you on schedule?

## Stick to the question.
- Make sure you know what the question asks you to do.
- Read the question carefully. Underline it or make notes on it. Go over it as many times as necessary to be sure you get it.
- After you plan, go back and read the question again. Ask yourself if your plan will result in a complete answer to the question.
- Before you revise, ask yourself, "Did I answer all parts of the test question?"

## Relax.
- Don't race or skip over any part of the process, such as reading the question carefully or revising and proofreading.
- Remember that you have practiced all of this before. You are ready!
- Remember that you have learned strategies for doing your best. They are going to help you now.

# PRACTICE TEST

Read this passage. Then answer the questions that follow.

## Firefighters to the Rescue

Firefighters perform some of the most important work in a community. They put out fires and perform many kinds of rescues. Often, they respond to medical emergencies. When someone in your town or city pulls an alarm or calls 911, chances are good that a firefighter will race to the scene.

There are many kinds of firefighting jobs. Not all of them involve fighting fires. Some firefighters teach members of their community about fire safety. Others investigate the causes of fires. They collect evidence from fires, interview witnesses, and write reports. Some firefighters work mainly as fire inspectors. They make sure buildings are safely built according to laws. Their work helps prevent fires.

Many firefighters do their jobs for free. Volunteer firefighters rush to work when an alarm is called in. They also spend some of their free time training, maintaining equipment, and doing other needed chores. Some firefighters are paid for full-time work. When they are not at the scene of a fire, they do other work in the community or at the firehouse. They may also be learning about new methods for fighting and preventing fires. Finally, some firefighters work on a "needs" basis. They

go to a fire when they are called, and they are paid only for that work. Many people who fight forest fires work this way. This is especially common during summers, when most forest fires occur.

Fighting a fire requires many different personality traits. One of the most important is the ability to think fast. A person has to respond quickly to an alarm. When a fire breaks out, there is often not a minute to lose. The unique problems of each emergency can require different solutions. A firefighter should also be in good physical shape. Quick thinking and quick action often go together.

Firefighters need specialized knowledge and training. They have to become familiar with all the equipment and learn to use it well. For example, they have to use equipment ranging from tower ladders to safety lines. They have to understand how pumper trucks and high-pressure hoses work. They have to develop knowledge of different causes and kinds of fires.

At the scene of a fire, firefighters have to stay calm. They must think and act under pressure. A firefighter may have only a few moments to save someone trapped in a building. In such a situation, a roof could collapse. Walls could cave in. Smoke could become deadly.

A firefighter also has to have excellent people skills. Firefighters have to know how to get terrified people to trust them. A firefighter also has to work well as a member of a team.

Some firefighters take great risks to help save people and property. At times, they are injured, often from smoke. Some pay the ultimate price. Still, firefighters go bravely forward to do their job no matter what the risk.

**1** What are the three traits that a firefighter should have? Answer the question in two or three sentences.

_____

_____

_____

_____

**2** What are three different jobs that firefighters do? Answer the question in two or three sentences.

_____

_____

_____

_____

**3** Read this test question. Then plan, write, revise, and edit your answer on the pages that follow.

> Firefighters are important members of a community. The work they do saves people, pets, homes, and other property. Do you think you have what it takes to be a firefighter? If so, what kind of firefighting job or role would you want? Write an essay stating your opinion about firefighting as a possible career or volunteer activity. Your response should include at least three paragraphs.

# Prewriting

Underline or mark up the test question as you wish. Then use the rest of this page to plan your response. Choose a graphic organizer to arrange your ideas.

_____

_____

_____

_____

_____

_____

_____

_____

_____

_____

_____

_____

_____

_____

_____

_____

_____

_____

_____

_____

_____

_____

# Drafting

Use this page to write your draft.

_____

_____

_____

_____

_____

_____

_____

_____

_____

_____

_____

_____

_____

_____

_____

_____

_____

_____

_____

_____

_____

_____

_____

**Drafting**

# Revising and Editing

Use this page to make your revisions. Then edit your work.

_____

_____

_____

_____

_____

_____

_____

_____

_____

_____

_____

_____

_____

_____

_____

_____

_____

_____

_____

_____

Practice Test

# Publish

Write your final copy on the page below. Then show it to your teacher.

_____

_____

_____

_____

_____

_____

_____

_____

_____

_____

_____

_____

_____

_____

_____

_____

_____

_____

_____

_____

_____

_____

**Publish**

# Editing

Edit this essay for mistakes. Write your corrections on the essay using standard proofreading marks.

My neighbor abigail Levy has been a volunteer firefighter in our town since 1991. Wanting to be a good member of her community. She first thought about volunteering in her son's elementary school. Than one of her friends told her that Springfield needed more volunteer firefighters. So, she went to see what it was all about.

Ms. Levy learned that, in springfield, firefighters get called more often for medical problems than for fires. They fight fires, too but often more they go out because someone is injured or having a heart attack. At first, Ms. Levy didn't know if she wanted to join or not. The firefighters said she should try out the training coarse. It was at their fire academy and then decide.

Ms. Levy did the ten-week course.  She learned about fire safety. She learned about fire equipment. She learned many rescue techniques. Read hundreds of pages! She also had to do a lot of exercises that she still does now. After she passed the course, she decided to serve her community. She decided to serve as a firefighter. Ms Levy says she also likes having a car with a flashing red light on top!

# HANDBOOK

## Capitalization

- Capitalize the first word of a sentence.

  **T**he sun is shining.

- Capitalize names and initials of people.

  **T**racy **G**. **P**eters   **U**ncle **H**enry   **M**ayor **S**oto

- Capitalize people's titles when they are used as part of the name.

  **M**s. **C**ourtney **E**vans   **S**. **J**enkins **J**r.

- Capitalize the names of days, months, places, and holidays.

| Days | Months | Places | Holidays |
|---|---|---|---|
| Wednesday | April | Brook Hill Middle School | Valentine's Day |
| Friday | June | Arizona | Memorial Day |
| Monday | November | Washington, D.C. | Thanksgiving |

- Do NOT capitalize the names of the seasons.

  winter, fall, spring, summer

## Punctuation

### End Marks

- A statement ends with a period: Pine trees stay green all year**.**

- A question ends with a question mark: Did you finish your math**?**

- An exclamation ends with an exclamation point: What a great movie**!**

### Commas

- Use a comma between the parts of a compound sentence. Place the comma before the word *and, but,* or *or.*

  A cold wind whistled**, but** the cabin remained warm and cozy.

- Use commas between words or phrases in a series.

  We packed tuna sandwiches**,** pickles**,** and apple juice.

- Use a comma between the day and year in a date: February 11**,** 2006

- Use a comma between a city and state: Memphis**,** Tennessee

## Apostrophes

- Make a singular noun possessive by adding an apostrophe and -s.

    the boss**'s** desk        a child**'s** toy

- When a plural noun ends in s, make it possessive by adding just an apostrophe. When a plural noun does not end in s, make it possessive by adding an apostrophe and -s.

    two students**'** reports        children**'s** books

- Use an apostrophe to show where letters are missing in a contraction:

    has + not = hasn't (*o* is missing)        I + am = I'm (*a* is missing)

## Quotation Marks

- Use quotation marks before and after a person's exact words.

    Sam said, **"**Anya forgot her lunch.**"**

## Titles

- Capitalize the first word, last word, and every important word in a title. Use quotation marks for titles of short works.

    article: **"How to Make a Kite"**

    short story: **"The Lion and the Mouse"**

    poem: **"A Cat"**

    Underline or use italics for longer works.

    book: <u>Shiloh</u> or *Shiloh*

    newspaper: <u>The Boston Globe</u> or *The Boston Globe*

# Grammar and Usage

## Subject-Verb Agreement

- When you use an action verb in the present tense, add the ending -s or -es to the verb if the subject is a singular noun or a singular pronoun (but not if the subject is either *I* or *you*).

    she swims        Amy swims

- Do not add -s or -es to the verb if the subject is plural, *I,* or *you.*

    Amy and Lori swim        the girls swim        I swim        you swim

# Subject-Verb Agreement with Forms of *be*

- With a singular noun subject, use *is* for the present tense and *was* for the past tense.

  Charles **is** here.    The weather **was** sunny last weekend.

- With a plural noun or a compound subject, use *are* for the present tense and *were* for the past tense.

  The students **are** late.    Luis and Eric **were** at the game yesterday.

- Use the correct form of *be* with a singular or plural pronoun subject.

| Present Tense | | Past Tense | |
|---|---|---|---|
| Singular | Plural | Singular | Plural |
| I **am** | we **are** | I **was** | we **were** |
| you **are** | you **are** | you **were** | you **were** |
| he, she, *or* it **is** | they **are** | he, she, *or* it **was** | they **were** |

## Irregular Verbs

The verbs below and many others are called irregular because their past-tense forms do not end in *ed*. Use the correct past-tense forms of irregular verbs.

| Present | Past | Past Participle |
|---|---|---|
| is | was | (has) been |
| begin | began | (has) begun |
| bring | brought | (has) brought |
| choose | chose | (has) chosen |
| come | came | (has) come |
| fly | flew | (has) flown |
| go | went | (has) gone |
| have | had | (has) had |
| know | knew | (has) known |
| make | made | (has) made |
| run | ran | (has) run |
| say | said | (has) said |
| speak | spoke | (has) spoken |
| swim | swam | (has) swum |
| take | took | (has) taken |
| wear | wore | (has) worn |
| write | wrote | (has) written |

## Subject and Object Pronouns

Pronouns have different subject and object forms. Use the subject form as the subject of a sentence. Use the object form after an action verb or after a preposition such as *of, to, for,* or *about.* The pronouns *you* and *it* have only one form.

| Subject Pronouns | |
|---|---|
| Singular | Plural |
| I | we |
| he | they |
| she | |

| Object Pronouns | |
|---|---|
| Singular | Plural |
| me | us |
| him | them |
| her | |

Wrong: Sara and **me** are here.

Correct: Sara and **I** are here.

Wrong: Don and **her** like chess.

Correct: Don and **she** like chess.

Wrong: Ann told Gina and **I**.

Correct: Ann told Gina and **me**.

Wrong: Give the pens to **he** and **I**.

Correct: Give the pens to **him** and **me**.

## Naming Yourself Last

When you speak of yourself and another person, name yourself (I or me) last.

**Roger** and **I** are neighbors.          Grandpa wrote to **Simon** and **me**.

## Possessive Pronouns

Use these possessive pronouns before a noun to show ownership.

| Singular | Plural |
|---|---|
| my | our |
| your | your |
| his, her, its | their |

Someone took **her** and **my** seats.

Use these possessive pronouns when a noun does not follow.

| Singular | Plural |
|---|---|
| mine | ours |
| yours | yours |
| his, her, its | theirs |

These seats are **hers** and **mine.**

## Tricky Words

Some words are often confused. Remember to use these words correctly.

| | |
|---|---|
| **a/an** | Use *a* before a consonant sound. Use *an* before a vowel sound.<br>     Wrong: **a** orange     Correct: **an** orange |
| **can/may** | In a question, use *can* to ask if something is possible. Use *may* to ask if something is allowed.<br>     Wrong: **Can** I borrow your pen?<br>     Correct: **May** I borrow your pen? |
| **good/well** | Use *good* only as an adjective. Use *well* as an adverb unless you are describing someone's state of health.<br>     Wrong: He pitches **good.**<br>     Correct: He pitches **well.** He is a **good** pitcher.<br>     Wrong: I have a cold and don't feel **good.**<br>     Correct: I have a cold and don't feel **well.** |
| **have/of** | Use *have* or *'ve* after words such as *could*, *should*, and *would*. Do not use *of*.<br>     Wrong: I could **of** gone.<br>     Correct: I could **have** gone. I could**'ve** gone. |
| **hear/here** | *Hear* means "to be aware of sound":  I **hear** music.<br>(*Hear* contains *ear!*)<br>*Here* means "in this place": Put your bags **here.** |
| **its/it's** | *Its* means "belonging to it": The dog wagged **its** tail.<br>*It's* means "it is": **It's** raining. |
| **than/then** | *Than* is a word for comparing: Today is hotter **than** yesterday.<br>*Then* means "at that time" or "next":<br>     Raise one arm and **then** the other. |
| **their/there/<br>they're** | *Their* means "belonging to them": They ate **their** dinner.<br>*There* means "in that place": **There** you are! Sit over **there.**<br>*They're* means "they are": **They're** the fastest runners. |
| **to/too/two** | *To* means "toward" or "for the purpose of":<br>     Go **to** the park **to** play.<br>*To* can also be part of a verb form: She likes **to** skate.<br>*Too* means "more than enough" or "also":<br>     I ate **too** much. You did, **too.**<br>*Two* means "the sum of 1 + 1": The cat had **two** kittens. |
| **who's/whose** | *Who's* means "who is": **Who's** coming to the party?<br>*Whose* is the possessive form of *who*:<br>     I don't know **whose** hat this is. |
| **your/you're** | *Your* means "belonging to you": Put on **your** jacket.<br>*You're* means "you are": **You're** late for the bus. |

# Proofreading Symbols

| Symbol | Meaning | Example |
|---|---|---|
| ∧ | Add letters or words. | List ideas ∧ your topic. *(about)* |
| ⊙ | Add a period. | That is not true ⊙ |
| ≡ | Capitalize a letter. | R2-D2 and c̲-3PO are loyal. |
| ⊃ | Close up space. | They form friend⌣ships. |
| ∧ | Add a comma. | There are robots today ∧ but they are different. |
| / | Make a capital letter lowercase. | The Ȓobots today are different. |
| ¶ | Begin a new paragraph. | ¶ Real robots look like machines. |
| ꝫ | Delete letters or words. | Real robots look like reꝫal machines. |
| ∾ | Switch the position of letters or words. | The robots are today like machines. |

# Notes